WRITING IN THE DISCIPLINES

Third Edition

Harcourt Brace College Publishers
Fort Worth Philadelphia San Diego New York Orlando Austin San Antonio
Toronto Montreal London Sydney Tokyo

CREDITS

"Abortion's Grim Alternatives," by Jacqueline H. Plumez reprinted from the *New York Times.* Copyright © 1988 by the New York Times Company. Reprinted by permission.

"The Italian Family: 'Stronghold in a Hostile Land'" reprinted from the *Holt Handbook,* 2nd ed., by Laurie Kirzner and Stephen Mandell. Copyright © 1989, 1986 by Holt, Rinehart and Winston, Inc.

"The Study of Fossil Flowers" reprinted from *Writing Research Papers Across the Curriculum,* 2nd ed., by Susan Hubbuch. Copyright © 1989 by Holt, Rinehart and Winston, Inc.

ISBN: 0–15–502538–4

Copyright © 1995 by Harcourt Brace & Company

Address editorial correspondence to:
Harcourt Brace Collge Publishers
301 Commerce Street, Suite 3700
Fort Worth, TX 76102

Address orders to:
Harcourt Brace & Company
6277 Sea Harbor Drive
Orlando, FL 32887
1-800-782-4479 outside Florida
1-800-433-0001 inside Florida

PRINTED IN THE UNITED STATES OF AMERICA

6 7 8 9 0 1 2 3 4 095 9 8 7

CONTENTS

PREPARING TO WRITE
FOR RESEARCH

IDENTIFYING A RESEARCH QUESTION
OR FORMING A HYPOTHESIS

In all disciplines, research is conducted to answer questions that someone wants answered. Consequently, when you as a student receive a writing assignment involving research, you must first identify the explicitly posed or the underlying question and then conduct research to answer it. The more sharply focused the question is, the more focused the response will be. If the assignment is fairly open and does not express a question, you will need to identify a question that you would like to have answered or that you think someone else would like to have answered. As you go through your notes on classwork, readings, and other sources, try to identify such a question. The answer to this question will be your paper's thesis statement.

Some scientific research begins with a question, and some begins with a tentative answer to a research question, which researchers call a hypothesis. If you begin with a question, the purpose of your research and subsequent paper will be to answer the question. If you begin with a statement that is a tentative answer to your question (a hypothesis in the sciences), the purpose of your research and paper will be to prove or disprove this statement.

ANSWERING A RESEARCH QUESTION
OR SUPPORTING A HYPOTHESIS

The various disciplines require you to answer your question or support your hypothesis with different types of research. Some questions, particularly those in the humanities, may be answered by library research; however, others will require methods of data collection like field research, case studies, analyses of statistics, and questionnaires.

1

Once you have determined the type of research you need to conduct and either located your sources or designed your tools for data collection, you must think critically. Ask yourself how relevant, valid, and accurate your sources are. If your sources are not believable, your readers will question your credibility as a researcher and the argument you will develop. Therefore, as you choose your research materials—and later, as you take notes—you need to make judgments about the credibility of sources.

TAKING NOTES

Whether you are a student of humanities, social science, natural science, or business, you will find note taking an important part of preparation for writing. Once you have mastered note-taking skills, you can apply them to writing assignments in any discipline.

Whenever you have a writing assignment or anticipate getting one, determine the questions the assignment is asking or will ask you to answer. Then begin to take notes on relevant material: observations, interviews, and textbook and library readings.

For instance, when you are reading a book or article, survey it, checking the headings and subheadings in the table of contents, and especially the index, for subjects you need to read carefully or to skim. As you read, underline and annotate sources whenever possible, and then take notes on index cards. Concentrated reading can help you narrow your focus still further as you see connections among ideas and develop new perspectives. As you read and take notes, you will move toward a thesis. This thesis will answer the stated or implied question behind your assignment and become the statement that your paper will support.

MAKING NOTE CARDS

Using index cards may seem cumbersome, but their advantages become obvious when you go about arranging and rearranging material. Often you do not know where you will use a particular piece of information or whether you will use it at all. You will be constantly rearranging ideas, and the flexibility of index cards makes adding and deleting information and experimenting with different sequences possible. Students who take notes in a notebook or on a tablet find that they spend as much time untangling their notes as they do writing their paper.

At the top of each card, *include a short heading* that relates the information on your card to your area of interest. Later, this heading may help you make your outline.

Each card should *accurately identify the source* of the information you are recording. These sources may be media, conversations or interviews, records, articles, or books. You need not include the complete citation, but you must include enough information to identify your source. "Wilson 72," for example, would send you back to your bibliography card carrying the complete documentation for *Patriotic Gore* by Edmund Wilson. For a book with more than one author, or for two books by the same author, you need a more complete reference. "Glazer & Moynihan 132" would suffice for *Beyond the Melting Pot* by Nathan Glazer and Daniel Patrick Moynihan. "Terkel, *Working* 135" would be necessary if you were using more than one book by Studs Terkel.

Here is one good note-card format. It illustrates notes taken from a book, but the format is applicable to all types of note taking.

	Art Style & Self Image	*Short heading*
Author, page	Alschuler 260	
Note	Children's view of themselves in society is reflected by their art style. A cramped, crowded art style using only a portion of the paper shows their limited role. The society consists of home, school, and friends.	

As you take notes on note cards, you can do several things that will make the actual writing of your paper easier.

Put only one note on each card. If one card contains several different points, you will not be able to try out different ways of arranging those points.

Include everything now that you will need later to understand your note. You might think, for instance, that this makes sense:

```
Peyser--four important categories of new music
```

But in several weeks you will not remember what those four categories were. They should have been listed on your card.

Put an author's comments into your own words whenever possible. Word-for-word copying of information is probably the most inefficient way to take notes. Occasionally you will want to copy down a particularly memorable statement or the exact words of an expert on your topic, and such quotations can strengthen your paper. But in your paper, for the most part, you will summarize and paraphrase your source material, adding your own observations and judgments. Putting information into your own words now keeps you from relying too heavily on the words of others or producing a paper that is a string of quotations rather than a thoughtful interpretation and analysis of ideas.

Remember to record your own observations and reactions. As you read your sources, get into the habit of writing down all the ideas—comments, questions, links with other sources, apparent contradictions, and so on—that occur to you. If you do not, you will probably forget them. But be sure to bracket your own reactions and observations so you will not confuse them with the author's material.

Indicate what kind of information is on your note card. If you copy an author's exact words, place them in quotation marks. If you use an author's ideas but not the exact words, do not use quotation marks. (Do not forget, however, to identify your source.) Finally, if you write down your own ideas, enclose them in brackets ([ ]). This system helps you avoid confusion—and plagiarism.

The student who wrote this note card was exploring the way the press portrayed President Richard Nixon during the Watergate crisis. Note that he has included only one note on his card, that both his note and its source are as complete as possible, and that he has clearly identified the first sentence as a summary ("The authors say . . . ") and the other comments as his own.

```
                                    Watergate

Woodward & Bernstein 366

     The authors say that by the summer of
1973 both Alexander Haig and Henry
Kissinger urged Richard Nixon to cut his
ties with his aides. [Is there any
evidence of this? What sources support
this? Seems doubtful.]
```

Quotation Note Cards

You *quote* when you copy an author's remarks just as they appear in your source, word for word, including all punctuation, capitalization, and spelling. When recording quotations, enclose all words that are not your own within quotation marks and identify your source with appropriate documentation. Check carefully to make sure that you have not inadvertently left out quotation marks or miscopied material from your source.

```
                              Matterhorn Accident

Whymper 393

     "Others may tread its summit-snows,
but none will ever know the feelings of
those who first gazed upon its marvelous
panorama, and none, I trust, will ever be
compelled to tell of joy turned into grief
and of laughter into mourning."
```

Paraphrase Note Cards

A *paraphrase* is a detailed restatement, in your own words, of the content of a passage. In it you not only present the main points of your source, but also retain their order and emphasis as well. A paraphrase will often include brief phrases quoted from the original to convey its tone or viewpoint. When you write a paraphrase, you should present only the author's ideas and keep your own interpretations, conclusions, and evaluations separate.

You paraphrase when you need detailed information from specific passages of a source but not the author's exact language. For this reason paraphrase is especially useful when you are presenting technical material to a general audience. It can also be helpful for reporting complex material or a particularly intricate discussion in easily understood terms. Although the author's concepts may be essential, the terms in which they are described could be far too difficult for your readers to follow. In such cases paraphrase enables you to give a complete sense of the author's ideas without using his or her words. Paraphrase is also useful when you want to convey the sense of a section of a work of literature or a segment of dialogue.

> **Original:**   Tyndall, <u>Hours of Exercise</u> (on the advantage of using a rope while mountain climbing):
>
> Not to speak of the moral effect of its presence, an amount of help upon a dangerous slope that might be measured by the gravity of a few pounds is often of incalculable importance.

```
                                        Ropes

 Tyndall 289

       Aside from its psychological effect,
 a rope can be extremely important when a
 slight steadying pressure is necessary.
```

Summary Note Cards

Unlike a paraphrase, which is a detailed restatement of a source, a summary is a general restatement, in your own words, of the meaning of a passage. Always much shorter than the original, a summary provides an overview of a piece of writing, focusing on the main idea. Because of its brevity, a summary usually eliminates the illustrations, secondary details, and asides that characterize the original. Like a paraphrase, a summary does not contain your interpretations, conclusions, or evaluations.

You summarize when you want to convey a general sense of an author's ideas to your readers. Summary is a useful technique when you want to record the main idea, but not the specific points or the exact words, of something that you have read. Because it need not follow the order or emphasis of a source, summary enables you to relate an author's ideas to your topic in a way that paraphrase and quotation do not.

```
                                              Ropes

   Tyndall 289-90

        In the 1800s, climbers thought ropes
   would help prevent falls by steadying
   mountain climbers who had lost their
   balance. However, the rope could be fatal
   to all tied to it if a climber actually
   fell.
```

Computer Note Taking

More and more researchers are beginning to save their notes on computer files. Sometimes this is done in the course of preparing an annotated bibliography. This task simplifies the preparation of your final paper greatly as it is often possible to copy sections from your notes into the main body of your paper. When you enter your notes into a "notes file" on computer, try to visualize your screen as an index card. Be sure to enter the complete bibliographic citation in the proper format. If you do so, you can assemble all the citations from your notes to prepare the bibliography.

ORGANIZING IDEAS

As you take notes, you need to organize your information into categories, each of which should be unified by a topic sentence that advances your argument. Each topic sentence will be supported by specific details and examples culled from your research. For instance, a sociological description of the "working mother" might provide these particulars: age 34; 81.6 percent employed with a household income of $40,000; interested in buying self-improvement, career guidance, jewelry, and beauty aids. These facts and figures can help to support a general point you may wish to make about the working mother.

Papers in all academic disciplines often include the following components.

1. An introduction in which you pose a research question and state your thesis.

2. A short review of literature describing the work of others out of which your research question grew.

3. Evidence to support your thesis.

4. Acknowledgment of opposing points of view and an explanation of how they differ from your point of view.

5. A conclusion which restates your thesis and summarizes your research.

This general arrangement covers a wide array of papers. Suppose, for instance, you were arguing the benefits to children of having a working mother. After using an interesting anecdote or example or statistic that had appeared in a newspaper, you could state the following thesis: "Children of working mothers often develop better social skills and greater financial responsibility as a result of their experiences in child care." This thesis could be followed by a narrative paragraph describing the available information on the development of children of working mothers. You would then go on to break down your supporting argument into its major parts. After supporting each aspect of your thesis with evidence, you can present opposing points of view and show their shortcomings. Then, restate your thesis in your conclusion.

All academic disciplines rely on certain familiar patterns of organizing material. *Comparison and contrast* is one such standard method of arranging ideas. In comparison and contrast, you bring together the similarities and dissimilarities of the subjects you are writing about to support a particular statement. The following paragraph from a sociology textbook supports the statement "Mexican-Americans have faced a great deal of prejudice and discrimination" by comparing and contrasting their experiences to those of blacks and Anglos.

> Clearly Mexican-Americans have faced a great deal of prejudice and discrimination. Like blacks, Mexican-Americans were segregated in restaurants, housing, schools, public facilities, and so on. They were frequently the victims of violence, which included beatings by police and servicemen. Today, the effects of the prejudice and discrimination directed against Mexican-Americans can still be seen. For instance, they

are more likely than Anglos to hold blue-collar jobs with a large number in service jobs such as janitors. Their unemployment rate averages about six points more than that for Anglos. Their median family income is only about 74 percent of the income of Anglo families. Mexican-Americans are more likely than both blacks and Anglos to experience job layoffs and cutbacks in work time. About 36 percent of the teenagers drop out of school, which is more than twice the rate for Anglo teenagers and almost double the rate for black teenagers (from Daniel M. Curran and Claire H. Renzetti, *Social Problems: Society in Crisis*, Boston: Allyn and Bacon, 1987).

Often information is organized in the order in which it occurs or in the order in which a procedure is carried out. For instance, a history paper might be organized *chronologically*, following the order in which certain historical battles were fought; a section of a scientific paper might be organized as a *process*, following the step-by-step procedure of a scientific experiment or describing a natural process such as digestion. Other familiar patterns of organizing ideas include *cause and effect* and *classification*.

ASSIGNMENTS IN ACADEMIC WRITING

Academic disciplines share certain assignments. For instance, in any discipline you may be required to write a literature survey, an abstract, or a proposal. In addition, each discipline has certain assignments—laboratory reports and case studies, for example—that are particular to it.

The most common assignments in college writing ask you to analyze a problem, a situation, or a work such as a literary text. The result is analytic papers in which you research a specific problem, gather data related to that problem, and propose specific solutions or applications of your solutions. These assignments usually require original thought, a clear statement of the problem, and suggested solutions. Most academic papers require research whether it is done in the library or the laboratory. Here is a research assignment from a marketing class.

Provide your classmates with a list of subsidiaries owned by a parent corporation. Example: General Electric owns RCA, RCA owns Avis Car Rentals and Random House Publishers, Random House owns Harlequin, and so on. Take a survey of the major companies with which your fellow students have had negative or positive experiences, including the number of times they have dealt with a company and what the results of their dealings have been. Can you make any generalizations about major conglomerates and their subsidiaries and how they affect the ordinary consumer? Should Congress pass laws that restrict the size of the companies? Write a research paper for your congressional representative explaining why he or she should support or reject such legislation.

Here is an English assignment that requires you to research dialects of English.

Write or tell a story about the area in which you grew up. Analyze your story to see whether you have used localized idiomatic phrases. Do your classmates understand them? Are there phrases they have used that you cannot understand? Can you define the particular dialect you are using? After doing some library research, write a paper for an audience of foreign students about how English usage varies across the United States.

Other assignments may require you to gather information about an area and its culture. For instance, in history you may be asked to gather information about the Tigua Indians; in political science you may be asked to talk to county officers or other local politicians. In these cases you will report on your findings. Writing a coherent paper requires focusing on a single idea and gathering specifics and details to support it.

RESEARCH SOURCES

The reference section of any library is the best place to find general research sources. The reference section of the library contains sources as diverse as encyclopedias, atlases, quotation books, and bibliographies as well as information that indicates where you actually find other material. In addition to the library's catalog, the reference section contains indexes, bibliographies, and computerized materials that can tell you where to find material on the research topic of your choice. One way to start your research is to browse in the subject section of your catalog. If you cannot find your topic in the subject section,

search *The Library of Congress Subject Headings*, which lists the
various names under which a subject might be listed.

GENERAL LIBRARY SOURCES

The following list is a guide to some of the major sources—
indexes, encyclopedias, bibliographies, and other library materials—that you can use to find general research information.

Indexes
Biography Index
Government Documents Index
Magazine Index
New York Times Index
Public Affairs Information Services Index
Reader's Guide to Periodical Literature
Wall Street Journal Index
Washington Post Index

Encyclopedias
Academic American Encyclopedia
Encyclopedia Americana
Encyclopaedia Britannica
Micropaedia
Propaedia
The New Columbia Encyclopedia
The Random House Encyclopedia

Bibliographies
Books in Print
The Bibliographic Index
The Subject Guide to Books in Print
Paperbound Books in Print

Other Sources
Dissertation Abstracts International
Editorials on File
Monthly Catalog of United States Government Publications
Historical Atlas
Encyclopaedia Britannica World Atlas
Facts on File
Statistical Abstracts
World Almanac

GENERAL DATABASES FOR COMPUTER SEARCHES

In many cases computerized searching makes research much faster and provides the option of combining key words (or *descriptors*) with author and title information to find exact citations. For instance, you may know only that Fredric Jameson has written an article on third-world literature, but not where it has been published or the exact title or contents. Since the article is about literature, you decide to search a literature database which yields various titles by Fredric Jameson. Matching the titles found with the key words "Third-world Literature," you find the following: Jameson, Fredric, "World Literature in an Age of Multinational Capitalism," in *The Current in Criticism* edited by Clayton Koelb and Virgil Lokke.

Some of the most widely used general databases include the *Magazine Index, Dissertation Abstracts Online, Biography Index, Books in Print, GPO Monthly Catalog, Newsearch, National Newspaper Index, New York Times Index, Marquis Who's Who,* and the *Reader's Guide to Periodical Literature.*

It is important to remember that although many databases have a print counterpart, some are available only on-line.

CD-ROM is a rapidly expanding new technology for database searching which is available in many libraries. Many indexes that are available in a print version are now offered on CD-ROM. CD-ROM offers a cost savings over on-line database searching and more flexibility than searching print indexes.

DOCUMENTING SOURCES

Documentation is the acknowledgment of what you have derived from a source and exactly where in that source you found your material. Not all fields use the same style of documentation. The most widely used formats are those advocated by the Modern Language Association (MLA), *The Chicago Manual of Style* (CMS), and the American Psychological Association (APA). In addition, the sciences, engineering, and medicine have their own formats. Before writing a paper in any of these areas, you should ask your instructor what style of documentation you should use and then follow it consistently throughout your paper (see "Overview of Documentation Styles: Books," p. 257).

WHAT TO DOCUMENT

You must document all materials that you borrow from your sources. Documentation enables your readers to identify your sources and to judge the quality of your work. It also encourages them to look up the books and articles that you cite. Therefore, you should carefully document the following kinds of information:

1. direct quotations
2. summaries or paraphrases of material from your sources
3. opinions, judgments, and original insights of others
4. illustrations, tables, graphs, and charts that you get from your sources

The references in your text should clearly point a reader to the borrowed material and should clearly differentiate your ideas from the ideas of your sources.

WHAT NOT TO DOCUMENT

Common knowledge, information that you would expect most educated readers to know, need not be documented. You can assume, for instance, that undocumented information that appears in several sources is generally known. You can also safely include facts that are widely used in encyclopedias, textbooks, newspapers, and magazines, or on television and radio. Even if the information is new to you, as long as it is generally accepted as fact, you need not indicate your source. However, information that is in dispute or that is credited to a particular person should be documented. You need not, for example, document the fact that the Declaration of Independence was signed on July 4, 1776, or that Josiah Bartlett and Oliver Wolcott signed it. However, you do have to document a historian's analysis of the document, or a particular scholar's recent discoveries about Josiah Bartlett.

As you can see, when to document is sometimes a matter of judgment. As a beginning researcher, you should document any material you believe might need acknowledgment, even if you suspect it might be common knowledge. By doing so, you avoid the possibility of plagiarism.

SUMMARY

In general, then, in all the papers you will be asked to write in college you will be required to express a central idea clearly and to ensure that the researched material relates to the thesis and is organized clearly. In many of the papers you will be asked to write, you will also be required to present as a central idea a well-reasoned argument, supported by research. The section that follows discusses argumentative writing.

DEVELOPING AN ARGUMENT

ARGUING AND PERSUADING

The world is filled with disagreement. One person likes pizza with anchovies; another finds anchovies disgusting. Your next-door neighbor claims the Red Sox won the World Series in 1954; you are sure they did not. One group adamantly promotes the "right to life"; another just as strongly favors the "pro-choice" stance. Each of these examples represents a difference of opinion, yet only one can be the basis for a reasoned argument requiring critical thinking.

Whether or not a person likes anchovies is a matter of personal preference. No matter how much you describe the delights of anchovies, you are not going to change the negative response of the confirmed anchovy-hater. Arguing with your neighbor who claims the Red Sox won the Series in '54 is equally fruitless. The statistics are a matter of record and can be easily discovered by checking a sports almanac. However, the question of whether abortion should remain legal can be argued rationally because it is not a simple matter of taste nor is its legitimacy a fact that can easily be discovered in a reference book. Making decisions about abortion requires weighing evidence, making judgments, and finally reaching a conclusion.

Whatever the discipline for which you are writing, neither matters of taste nor matters of fact are worthy topics for argument. Matters requiring judgments, on the other hand, may (and often should) be the subject of well-reasoned, carefully planned arguments. Consider, for example, the following article that first appeared on the editorial page of the *New York Times*.

Abortion's Grim Alternative

Jacqueline H. Plumez

Given that several Supreme Court justices are more than eighty years of age, George Bush will probably appoint enough justices during the next four years to make good his promise to outlaw most abortions. "I favor adoption," he has said. "Let them come to birth, and then put them in a family where there will be love."

Well, I favor adoption, too. For ten years, I have been researching adoption and writing positively about it. But I think that George Bush is naive to believe that adoption can replace abortion.

Outlawing abortion would unwittingly guarantee that millions of children would be raised by parents who do not want them. The price the country would pay to raise these unwanted children could financially and morally bankrupt us.

Abortion has not caused the shortage of adoptable babies. Ninety percent of adoptable infants are born out of wedlock, and today, there are 118 percent more illegitimate babies born each year than before abortion was legalized in 1973.

Furthermore, it is a false assumption that most women who are forced to bear unwanted children place them for adoption. Ninety-seven percent of unmarried women who give birth try to raise their babies themselves.

Even in the days when it was much less acceptable to be an unmarried mother, only 30 percent of the single women who gave birth placed their babies for adoption. And today, 20 percent of the women who have abortions are married women, who rarely place unwanted children for adoption.

Society and our social-welfare system are now overburdened by the number of unplanned children. It could be pushed to collapse if the current 1.6 million abortions per year become unwanted children. Twenty-three percent of America's babies are born out of wedlock—more than 878,000 illegitimate children a year. That figure could triple if abortion is criminalized.

Today, one in six teenage girls gets pregnant at least once before marriage, half of all welfare payments go to women who gave birth as teenagers, and half of all children in foster care were born out of wedlock. Studies clearly show that such mothers and children are likely to remain undereducated and live in poverty—in families that will form a huge and permanent underclass.

Contrary to George Bush's beliefs, when women give birth to unwanted children, love does not find a way. Unwanted pregnancies tend to yield unwanted children.

According to the American Psychological Association, "Unwanted childbearing has been linked to a variety of social problems, including divorce, poverty, child abuse, and juvenile delinquency. As adults, unwanted children are more likely to engage in criminal behavior, be on welfare, and receive psychiatric services."

I believe that George Bush is a kind man who wants children to grow up loved and wanted. I do too. That's why we both favor adoption. But I also believe that George Bush has not looked into the consequences of making abortion illegal. And that scares me.

Whether or not you agree with Jacqueline Plumez's view, you can see that she has argued carefully and thoughtfully to convince readers that her position is worthy of consideration. How does a writer conceive, plan, develop, draft, and revise an argument such as "Abortion's Grim Alternative"? Although we cannot know Plumez's exact process, the steps that follow explain how to write an argument using her essay as an example.

EXPLORING THE ISSUE
AND POSING THE QUESTION

In college courses, whether in the humanities, the social sciences, the sciences, or business, you may be assigned a debatable position to argue for or against; or you may be assigned an issue or question and asked to formulate your own position. (In the natural sciences, this position might be called a hypothesis.) In the professional world, issues arise naturally. A supervisor, after noting the rising number of on-the-job accidents, may, for instance, write a memo arguing that the company's current safety regulations need to be changed. Nevertheless, there are also many instances when work-related writing is assigned. Plumez's editor may have said, "We need a piece on abortion." She then would have faced the same situation as a student whose professor assigns a paper on a controversial issue in literature, sociology, biology, or business.

First, she had to consider what she already knew and thought. She had to explore her previous experiences and try to identify and evaluate her emotional responses as well as her rational reactions. Plumez almost certainly had some general thoughts about the issue before she began to sort through her options, but she also knew that, like most students facing a paper assignment, she had a limited amount of space in which to present her argument, and also like students, she was facing a deadline. She certainly could not cover, or even summarize, every facet of the enormously complex abortion issue. She may have chosen at this point to jot down a list of ideas that came into her mind, topics that related to abortion. Because she had previously researched and written a great deal on adoption, the term *adoption* would be likely to appear on her list, and this may have led her to the precise, narrowed focus of her article. (See "Research Sources," pp. 10, 35, 105, 159, and 209.) Of course, any number of other scenarios are possible. For instance, she may have discussed her assignment with a friend who reminded her of her expertise on adoption. Or she may have started some preliminary reading and noticed the quotation from former President Bush that she uses in her opening paragraph. His comment may have been the spark that encouraged her to put adoption and abortion together.

As you are narrowing, refining, and defining a position for argument in any academic discipline, consider the following approaches:

1. exploratory writing (listing, note taking, or freewriting, for example)

2. collaborative discussion (with a friend, a writing center consultant, or a group of classmates)

3. preliminary reading (broadly focused reading aimed at surveying the issue rather than gathering evidence; see "Taking Notes," p. 2)

EVALUATING THE AUDIENCE

Once Plumez decided on a focus for her article, the connection between adoption and abortion, she had to think about the audience for whom she was writing. As a professional writer, she would know that, as a group, *New York Times* readers tend to be liberal politically and reasonably well educated. Because of their liberal bias, they are likely to be at least somewhat receptive to what she is saying. Because they are well educated, they will be able to understand the significance of statistics and will not need extended explanations of references such as the opening comment on the U.S. Supreme Court. Plumez can make decisions about word choice, tone, and presentation of evidence based on her knowledge of her audience.

Although most papers written for a class have the instructor as the primary reader, other class members are often also part of the audience. As you consider the audience to whom you will be presenting your argument, you should ask the following questions:

1. Are your readers hostile, sympathetic, or neutral to your argument?

2. What is the education level of your readers?

3. What special knowledge of your topic can you expect from your readers?

Note: Although you present ideas differently to different audiences, you do not, of course, alter your basic stance. Once you have explored a topic thoroughly and arrived at what you believe to be the truth, you stand by your findings. What changes is the way you explain your beliefs, not the beliefs themselves.

FORMULATING THE THESIS

Once Jacqueline Plumez had decided that she would deal with the connection between adoption and abortion, and once she had considered her audience, her next logical step was to formulate her position to answer the question: "Should abortion remain legal?" After thinking about her subject, and perhaps doing more preliminary reading and discussing (this time focusing on her specific position), she may have decided on the point expressed in the final sentence of her second paragraph ". . . George Bush is naive to believe that adoption can replace abortion." This statement, then, is her "position"; she now needs to explore evidence to see whether or not she can support this position with a strong argument. (See "Answering a Research Question or Supporting a Hypothesis," p. 1.)

As you formulate your position, remember that this assertion will become your thesis.

Exercise

Consider the following example.

> Issue—The number of non-readers in the United States
> is in the millions and increasing.
>
> Question—How can elementary schools work to decrease
> the number of functionally illiterate citizens in the United
> States?
>
> Position (thesis)—Schools must give preeminence to
> reading and study and implement the best methods so
> that students may come to love reading.

For each of the following topics, define an issue, pose a question,
and develop a position.

> Gun-related deaths in the United States
> Noise pollution
> Child custody laws
> Capital punishment
> Health fads
> Credit ratings
> Child abuse
> Public art

GATHERING EVIDENCE

During the years Plumez researched and wrote about adoption,
she almost certainly used two important thinking strategies:
inductive reasoning and deductive reasoning. Anyone gathering
evidence to support an argument in any discipline (but
particularly in the social sciences and sciences) needs to be aware
of these patterns of logical thinking.

When you explore evidence through *inductive reasoning*, as is
customary in the natural and in some social sciences, you observe
many similar examples and then make a generalization based on
what you discovered. Plumez, for example, must have observed
many adoptive parents and adoptive children to have reached
the conclusions that led her "to write positively about" adoption.

She probably looked for specific behaviors and situations that she defined as positive and when she found them, noted the families that displayed those qualities as support for her theory.

Inductive reasoning, then, requires that you make observations of individuals and move to a general conclusion about the class to which those individuals belong. Plumez, for instance, might have moved from her observation of individual adoptive families to the general conclusion that adoption usually benefits both the adoptive parents and the child.

When you use inductive reasoning, it is important to remember these guidelines:

1. Pose a sharply focused question.

2. Observe a sufficiently large sample (interviewing two happy families—or even five or ten—would not allow for making generalizations about adoption).

3. Acknowledge and explain examples that do not support your generalization.

When you explore evidence through *deductive reasoning,* you follow a process that is just the reverse of inductive reasoning. When you use induction, you observe many examples and move to a new generalization. When you use deduction, you reason from a known principle to an unknown, from the general to the specific, or from a premise to a logical conclusion. You start with a generalization that is widely accepted and use that *assumption* as the basis for your argument. Of course, understanding your audience is very important when you write a deductive argument. In the United States, for instance, we can assume that most people value universal formal education (an assumption that is not true in some countries where school time for the lower classes is regarded as time away from the physical labor that supports poorer families' meager existence). Therefore, most readers in the United States would be willing to accept the premise that a practice that enhances education deserves consideration. Jacqueline Plumez might, then, have written a very different argument from the one that appears here. She might have begun by praising the value the United States places on universal education and then moved to a series of examples showing that unwed teenage mothers, who are more likely than other teenagers to remain uneducated, deserve that education just as much as any other legal residents. In formal terms, the argument would have looked like this:

Major premise: All legal residents of the United States are entitled to be formally educated.

Minor premise: Teenage unwed mothers discussed in this essay are legal residents of the United States.

Conclusion: Therefore, the teenage unwed mothers discussed in this essay are entitled to be formally educated.

Of course, the essay itself would not be as simple as the formal outline suggests. The deductive pattern of reasoning might lead, for example, to a conclusion suggesting ways alternative programs to educate unwed mothers could be developed.

When you use deductive reasoning it is important to remember these guidelines:

1. The major premise must be widely accepted by your audience as true.

2. The minor premise must be widely accepted by your audience as true.

3. The reasoning used to reach your conclusion must be logically sound (for instance, in the hypothetical example above, if the author had used examples of teenage mothers who lived in Bangladesh and Bolivia, then the conclusion would not have been valid because the minor premise would have been untrue).

The discussions of inductive and deductive reasoning give examples of *primary source evidence*—that is, evidence that is discovered through personally conducted observations, investigations, or experiments. When you use primary source evidence, you must convince your readers that your findings are sound by observing the following guidelines:

1. Explain the *process* of your investigation or the *design* of your experiment when this information is needed to make your conclusions credible.

2. Be specific about the *number* of instances you observed; the larger the number, the more convincing your evidence will be.

3. Demonstrate that examples you observe are *representative* (typical) and therefore worthy to serve as the basis for general inferences and conclusions.

4. Establish your expertise or *qualifications* for carrying out the investigation or experiment.

While many arguments make use of primary source evidence, most also use *secondary source evidence.* A high percentage of papers written for the courses in the various academic disciplines require use of such evidence. (See "Research Sources," pp. 10, 35, 105, 159, and 209.) Secondary source evidence comes from researching information someone else has gathered. You may find such information through conducting interviews, through watching documentary television programs or through reading. In her essay, Jacqueline Plumez makes frequent use of secondary source evidence. For example, she cites statistics to support several of her points, and she also quotes the American Psychological Association. When you are gathering secondary source evidence, observe the following guidelines:

1. *Pay close attention and take accurate notes:* In the case of interviews, making a recording (with the permission of the person interviewed) allows you to check your notes. If you have access to a VCR, the same is true for television documentaries. (Some television stations offer transcripts of certain programs, usually for a small fee.) With library periodicals or books, photocopying particularly important pages provides you with the option for a final accuracy check.

2. *Evaluate the expertise and possible biases of your sources:* You must be certain that individuals whose ideas you cite to support your arguments are respected in their fields, even by those who

disagree with their views. For instance, William F. Buckley, Jr., a conservative writer, has a solid reputation among people with widely divergent political views. A quotation from Buckley would certainly carry far more authority (even with someone who disagreed with him politically) than one from a writer in the *National Enquirer,* which is known for its sensational and highly inaccurate reporting. And even respected writers may have personal biases that are widely known and that therefore make their ideas less convincing than the views of a more objective source.

3. *Evaluate the accuracy of the information you gather:* A helpful way to evaluate accuracy is to consult more than one source on the same topic. If several sources confirm the same findings and report the same statistics (and if these sources are all well respected), you can be fairly certain the data you want to use are correct. Some statements, of course, cannot be tested for absolute accuracy, but you should weigh their validity by considering logical fallacies and assuring yourself that none of the writers you plan to cite has been guilty of fallacious reasoning.

DRAFTING THE ARGUMENT

Once you have gathered and evaluated your evidence, you then decide whether or not you can convincingly support your tentative thesis. If you cannot, you have two choices: You can modify or even discard your thesis (remember that the primary point of an argument is to discover and reveal the truth), or, if you believe that your thesis is valid, you can seek more evidence that you think will persuade your readers. When you have finally finished gathering evidence, you must decide how to use it most effectively in your written argument. Generally, evidence makes up the body of the argument while the introduction and conclusion serve other purposes. For this reason, many writers draft the body of their essay first and then work on their introduction and conclusion.

Understanding the primary purposes of each part of an argument provides a helpful overview of the process of writing a persuasive essay.

INTRODUCTION

The introduction of an argument may be a single paragraph or, as in Jacqueline Plumez's article, it may be composed of several paragraphs. In the opening section, you want to get your reader's attention, perhaps by using a significant quotation (as Plumez does). You also want to establish your credibility. Although not all arguments allow for the use of first person, when possible it is extremely useful to demonstrate your expertise in an area as Plumez does when she says, "For ten years, I have been researching adoption and writing about it positively." With this statement, she also suggests that she is not unfairly biased against adoption and that, in fact, she favors the process. Plumez does everything she can to establish a believable *persona*—that is, to demonstrate a writing personality her audience will see as thoughtful, rational, and fair-minded. As a writer develops a credible "self," he or she strives in the opening paragraphs of arguments to establish *common ground* (a body of shared assumptions) with the audience. By explaining her agreement with Bush on adoption, Plumez also aligns herself with those readers (the vast majority) who believe that adoption is a positive social institution. When readers hold values in common with a writer, they are more likely to listen to that writer with an open mind. In addition to capturing readers' interest and creating a favorable self-image, the opening of an argument should also suggest its direction. When Plumez says, "I think that George Bush is naive to believe that adoption can replace abortion," she indicates that her essay will argue for maintaining the legalization of abortion and that it will focus specifically on problems with the proposal that adoption replace abortion.

BODY

How you organize the body of your essay depends on several factors. (See "Organizing Ideas," p. 7.) One of the first choices you must make concerns whether you want to deal with *opposing claims* early in your essay, integrate them throughout your essay, or treat them in your conclusion. Plumez structures her essay by challenging opposing claims, offering evidence to support her challenges, and then establishing her own claims. First she discusses why adoption cannot be a replacement for abortion, offering statistics regarding illegitimate births and the behavior pattern of unwed mothers to explain her contention that abortion has not caused the shortage of adoptable babies. Only after she has dealt with the opposing claim concerning adoption does she provide additional reasons why she believes abortion must not be criminalized. Plumez's article, then, provides one possible pattern for the body of an argument:

1. Explain and refute opposing claims.

2. Introduce new evidence.

You may, instead, choose a different pattern. Consider, for example, these two possible variations:

1. Introduce and support your first point; explain and refute any claim opposing that point.

2. Introduce and support your second point; explain and refute any claim opposing that point.

or

1. Introduce and support all of your points.

2. Explain and refute opposing claims.

Sometimes, of course, your opponents have legitimate claims. In that case, you may choose to briefly acknowledge those points but move on quickly to show that those few legitimate claims do not validate the opponents' entire argument. Plumez, for instance, notes that Bush's pro-adoption stand is admirable, but she moves on to explain why that belief does not lead logically to his stand on abortion.

Argumentative papers in all academic disciplines require you to decide where and how you will refute opposing claims. In addition, you must also make other decisions about ordering evidence. For example, will you offer your strongest points first, hoping to win converts to your cause as soon as possible, or will you save the most important evidence for a powerful conclusion, hoping to leave readers with the point you consider most crucial firmly in mind? Neither decision is necessarily right or wrong, but it is certainly essential to evaluate your evidence so that you understand your strong points as well as your weaker points and use them to what you believe will be the best advantage.

You must also decide whether your argument will appeal primarily to the minds *(appeals to reason)* of your readers, or primarily to their feelings *(appeals to emotion)* or whether you will try to sway both their thoughts and their feelings. (Sometimes the term *persuasion* is applied to appeals primarily to emotions while *argument* is used to describe appeals to the mind. In reality, most essays in any discipline that aim to reveal what the writer believes to be true and to convince others to accept those ideas as true combine rational and emotional appeals.) Although emotional appeals are often thought of as somehow less worthy and less important than rational appeals, the two are usually equally powerful and equally deserving of consideration. We are, after all, human beings, and one important sign of our humanity is that we make choices based on our feelings as well as our thoughts. Of course, both rational and emotional appeals must be presented honestly. No one likes to feel duped, and if the members of your audience realize, for example, that you have manipulated statistics to appeal falsely to their minds, they will be just as disillusioned as they would be if you created exaggerated pictures of misery to incite their horror or fear with no purpose other than to gain profit (or power) for yourself. As you draft the body of your argument, stay aware of your appeals and make sure they are both valid and balanced. You do not want to project the image of an unthinking automaton who simply spits out charts and figures, but neither do you want to seem hysterical, shrill, or morbid.

CONCLUSION

Just as the introduction is worthy of concentrated effort and attention because it provides your readers with their first impression of you and your argument, your conclusion, too, must be carefully planned because it leaves the final image in your audience's mind. Although you may be tempted to simply summarize the points you have made in the body of your argument, it is usually wise to resist this temptation. Particularly if your argument is relatively short, your audience should be able to remember your main ideas as well as at least some of the evidence you have provided for support. In your final paragraphs, then, you want to offer something more than a simple review. Consider, for example, Plumez's last three paragraphs. First, she returns to her opening reference to George Bush, once again refuting his claim, yet doing it in a different way than she did in her introduction. She follows up her contention that "unwanted pregnancies tend to yield unwanted children" with a quotation from the American Psychological Association that projects distinctly undesirable effects of forced childbearing. Here Plumez does not simply restate earlier evidence suggesting that problems will occur for single mothers and for our social-welfare system if abortion is criminalized; instead she offers a final, powerful look at the probable fate of the unwanted who will be born. If she has any chance of convincing her audience to accept her views, this argument should be the most effective. Even people who are unconcerned with the fate of unwed mothers or the burdening of the social-welfare system may very well be moved by the picture of children doomed to grow up in the shadow of "poverty, child abuse, and juvenile delinquency." In her final paragraph, Plumez once again shows herself to be a rational, calm writer with no personal grudge against Mr. Bush: "I believe that George Bush is a kind man," she says. And when she adds that he is a person "who wants children to grow up loved and wanted," and that she does, too, she once again establishes common ground not only with Bush, but also with most readers who will certainly share those values. Only after this demonstration of mutual beliefs and only after a confirmation of her belief in adoption does Plumez go on to her controversial final statements: "But I also believe that George Bush has not looked into the consequences of making abortion illegal. And that scares me." She hopes, of course, that the evidence she has offered earlier in the essay will lead at least some of her readers to share her concern and her fear and to agree with her argument that abortion must remain legal.

When you are writing the conclusion of an argument, remember these guidelines:

1. Make certain your final comments follow logically from and are supported by the evidence you have provided in the body of your essay.

2. Consider various approaches for leaving a strong, final impression on your audience. For example, you might include

   - a relevant and memorable quotation
   - an especially convincing example or piece of evidence
   - a compelling statistic
   - a moving anecdote

3. Be sure that your conclusion does more than summarize; it should also evaluate, analyze, predict, or recommend.

4. Reaffirm your stance as a reasonable, thoughtful writer.

REVISING THE ARGUMENT

Drafting an argument does not, of course, assure that you have produced a finished copy. In most cases, the draft simply provides you with workable material that you must mold into the best possible essay to support your thesis and to convince your readers of its validity.

As you begin the revising (literally, the "re-seeing") process, one of the most effective—yet most difficult—approaches is to try to take on the feelings and thoughts of a hostile reader. Even though the audience for whom you are writing may be neutral or may favor your thesis, you will see the weak spots more quickly if you adopt the mindset of those who most adamantly oppose your argument. Since you have already researched opposing claims, you know some of the main points your opponents would make, but you have to go further. Now you have to imagine someone who does not agree with you, someone who is reading and responding to what you have written. How might that person attack your evidence? Can you anticipate his or her counterarguments? And, of course, most important, can you make any changes in your essay that will block those attacks or counterarguments?

Consider, for example, Jacqueline Plumez's article which has been used to demonstrate strategies for writing strong arguments. Here is a finished, published piece, yet even so there are questions opponents might raise. As a quick exercise in revision, reread "Abortion's Grim Alternative" and note objections you might raise or challenges you might make. For instance, in paragraph four, Plumez notes that 118 percent more illegitimate babies are now born out of wedlock than were in 1973 when abortion was legalized. Later in her essay she argues that abortion must remain legal in order to stop the number of illegitimate births. An opponent might ask Plumez whether she did not see a contradiction here. Since illegitimate births have *increased* following the legalizing of abortion, how can she suggest abortion as a solution? And how might Plumez have avoided that challenge if she had anticipated it? She might have noted that she was not proposing abortion as the only solution, or the best solution, to illegitimate births but that criminalizing abortion would certainly complicate the problem. Whether you agree or disagree with Plumez, your rereading no doubt led you to see other statements that her opponents might challenge. Are there ways Plumez could have changed her essay to answer those challenges? Or was she wise to ignore them and continue presenting her own evidence? Obviously no writer can provide minute explication of every piece of evidence; part of the revision process requires deciding where more explanation will strengthen what you have written and where more explanation will simply confuse or annoy the reader.

One question you may raise when evaluating Plumez's essay is why she does not fully document her sources. (See "Documenting Sources," p. 12.) She cites many statistics and quotes both former President Bush and the American Psychological Association, but she does not tell readers where she found this information. Every English course from elementary school through the graduate level teaches the importance of proper documentation, yet Plumez's article is typical of those published in newspapers and popular magazines. The answer to your question about documentation lies in the varying conventions of popular journalism and academic publishing. Papers that are written for classes or for scholarly journals require careful identification of sources for three reasons: Readers can evaluate the probable validity of your evidence by knowing its source, readers can consult your sources for further information or to examine the data in context, and readers can recognize your acknowledgment of using data compiled by others. Especially in an academic setting, acknowledging sources is essential to avoid the charge of plagiarism. (For proper documentation format, see "Documentation Formats," pp. 41, 114, 166, and 218.) Remember that different disciplines use different forms; check with your instructor to learn which you should follow.

As you revise an argumentative essay, consider the following guidelines:

1. Make certain your introduction catches the reader's attention and establishes the thesis of your argument.

2. Make certain you have organized your evidence effectively.

3. Make certain you have provided sufficient evidence to make your case convincing.

4. Make certain statistics and other data are accurate and are derived from respected sources.

5. Make certain you have not used unfounded emotional appeals.

6. Make certain your rational appeals are logical and valid (check your writing handbook).

7. Make certain you have anticipated and defused opposing claims.

8. Make certain you have established a credible writing persona.

9. Make certain your conclusion follows logically from the evidence you have presented.

10. Make certain you have proofread carefully.

TOPICS FOR
ARGUMENTATIVE WRITING

You will develop most arguments in response to a specific assignment or situation. The following list provides representative topics from various academic disciplines.

THE HUMANITIES

1. Consider three important decisions Lincoln made during the Civil War and present an argument explaining why you think those decisions did or did not prolong the war unnecessarily.

2. During World War II, press photographers were censored and were not allowed to show the full horror through pictures of dismembered bodies and other such results of battle. During the Korean and Vietnam conflicts such censorship was not in place. After investigating this issue, argue for the policy you favor.

3. Should freedom of speech include the right to burn the American flag? Is this a topic worthy of congressional debate and possibly a constitutional amendment? After reading the claims of people on both sides of this issue, write an argument defending your point of view.

THE SOCIAL SCIENCES

4. Many state governments support a lottery. Does this legalization of gambling represent a threat to the moral fabric of those states' citizens? Are state lotteries, in fact, encouraging false hopes and, worse, providing a breeding ground for the disease of compulsive gambling? Study the issue and offer an argument explaining your point of view.

5. Recent surveys suggest that many high school graduates do not know basic facts of geography, history, or literature, nor can they do simple math problems. Should nationwide "exit exams" be required, to assure that all

high school graduates have acquired a certain degree of "cultural literacy"? Investigate this topic and argue for the conclusion you reach.

6. Experts on childhood development disagree concerning the benefits of organized sports teams that begin with players as young as age 5. Investigate the physical as well as psychological benefits and detriments of organized sports for young children. Then write an essay arguing for or against participation on such teams.

7. Corporations are obligated to provide paternity leave as well as maternity leave. After researching this topic, argue for or against compensated leave time for new fathers.

THE SCIENCES

8. Some scientists have argued that the declining rate of childbearing among educated women will lead to a decline in the intelligence and productivity of the United States population. Do you agree? Investigate this question and then write an argument explaining your response.

9. What policies has your state implemented to address environmental concerns? Investigate this question and then decide whether or not you think the actions taken are sufficient. Write an argument defending your view.

10. Recent court cases show that patients and their families are increasingly seeking the right to make their own decisions about the use of life-support systems to sustain hopelessly terminal cases. Who should make the decision? Patients and/or their families? A judge? A doctor? After investigating this issue, write an argument explaining your recommendations.

A FINAL NOTE

In many of the papers you will be asked to write in college, you will be required to present a well-reasoned argument and to ensure that researched material supports that argument in a clearly identifiable pattern. However, each of the four broad disciplinary areas—the humanities, the social sciences, the sciences, and business—has its own particular research sources, paper formats, assignments, styles, and methods of documentation. The sections that follow discuss the differences in the four disciplinary areas.

WRITING IN THE HUMANITIES

The humanities include a variety of subjects, including art, music, literature, history, languages, and philosophy. Some of these disciplines use different documentation styles and special library sources.

RESEARCH SOURCES

Library research is an important part of study in many humanities disciplines. When you begin your research in any subject area, the *Humanities Index* is one general source you can turn to. There are also many specialized sources available as you continue your research process.

SPECIALIZED LIBRARY SOURCES

The following list represents some of the sources used often in the various humanities disciplines.

Art
>   *Art Index*
>   *Art Reproductions in Books*
>   *McGraw-Hill Encyclopedia of World Art*
>   *New Dictionary of Modern Sculpture*
>   *Oxford Companion to Art*

Drama
>   *New York Times Theatre Reviews*
>   *McGraw-Hill Encyclopedia of World Drama*
>   *Modern World Drama: An Encyclopedia*
>   *Oxford Companion to the Theatre*

Film
>   *Guide to Critical Reviews*
>   *International Index to Multimedia Information*

Lander's Film Reviews
New York Times Film Reviews

History
Cambridge Ancient History
Cambridge Medieval History
CRIS (Combined Retrospective Index to Journals in History, 1838–1974)
Great Events in History
Guide to Historical Literature
Harvard Guide to American History
Historical Abstracts (Europe)
New Cambridge Modern History

Language and Literature
Annual Bibliography of English Language and Literature
Biography Index
Book Review Digest
Book Review Index
Children's Literature Abstracts
Contemporary Authors
Current Biography
Essay and General Literature Index
LHUS (Literary History of the United States)
LLBA (Language and Language Behavior Abstracts)
MLA International Bibliography
Oxford Companion to American Literature
Oxford Companion to Classical Literature
Oxford Companion to English Literature
Princeton Encyclopedia of Poetry and Poetics
PMLA General Index
Salem Press Critical Surveys of Poetry, Fiction, Long Fiction, and Drama
Short Story Index
Webster's Biographical Dictionary
Twentieth Century Authors

Music
Grove's Dictionary of Music and Musicians
Harvard Dictionary of Music
Music Article Guide
Music Index

Philosophy
> *The Concise Encyclopedia of Western Philosophy and*
> *Philosophers*
> *Encyclopedia of Philosophy*
> *Philosopher's Index*

SPECIALIZED DATABASES FOR COMPUTER SEARCHES

Many of the print indexes that appear on the above list of specialized library sources are also available on-line. Some of the most helpful databases for humanities disciplines include *Humanities Index, Art Index, MLA Bibliography, Religion Index, Philosopher's Index, RILM Abstracts, Essay and General Literature Index, Artbibliographies Modern, Historical Abstracts,* the *LLBA Index,* and *Comprehensive Dissertation Abstracts.*

NON-LIBRARY SOURCES

Research in the humanities is not limited to the library. Historians may need to do oral interviews or archival work or consult papers collected in town halls, churches, or courthouses. Art majors may need to visit museums and galleries. Attending concerts is a legitimate form of field work for music majors.

Non-library sources can be important additions to a paper in any humanities discipline. For instance, in writing about history you not only study the events of the past, but you also interpret the information you collect. It is then up to you to defend your interpretation of those events. The following excerpt from a student's oral history interview was a valuable resource for her paper about Tigua Indians.

> Arturo Tapia, a registered Tigua Indian, recalls, "My daddy never used to say he was Tigua Indian . . . we never talked about it . . . other Indians never liked us and the white people never allowed us in their bars or stores. I have gone up to people and told them I am Tigua and they say, 'What a low class Indian,' or 'Them down there, the Mexicans, they sold out.'"

The student who recorded this interview chose to use it in her opening paragraph, to help introduce her paper's thesis.

The history of the Tiguas is full of misconceptions. The New Mexico version of the Tiguas' migration is that they fled with a Spanish party to El Paso during the Indian uprising of August 10, 1680, while the Tigua version of their migration is quite different. The New Mexico Indians have portrayed the Tiguas of Isleta as a "Judas Tribe" who turned against their own people to ally with the Spanish. Even today the Tiguas face discrimination from other Indians as well as from Whites and feel they are considered "low class" (Rosario).

ASSIGNMENTS IN THE HUMANITIES

THE RESPONSE STATEMENT

One assignment particular to the humanities is the response statement, in which you analyze and interpret your reactions to a work. In such a paper you are asked simply to express your personal reaction to a work such as Keats's "Ode to a Grecian Urn" or to a painting or to a concert you attended. Such an assignment requires you to write a first-person account of your feelings upon encountering a work and to account, if you can, for what influenced your response.

THE BOOK REVIEW

A book review summarizes or outlines a book and provides your evaluation of it. Book reviews are assigned in all the humanities disciplines, particularly literature, history, and philosophy, and in most cross-disciplinary humanities or general education sequences. Here is a sample book review from *World Literature Today*, Spring 1988.

Timothy Mo's novel *An Insular Possession* is a rather slow-moving account of British colonizers in the Far East. . . . Walter Eastman, one of the principal characters, calls himself, in a letter, a "philosopher of the verandah." Even the American characters are infected with British practices, as they are with loathing for their steamy surroundings and the natives.

What Mo does do beautifully is evoke that languid, steamy existence. In his delicate and beautifully written descriptions he shows the power of the English language in the hands of non-native English-speaking ex-colonials. His characters O'Rourke and Eastman are painters, metaphors for the author himself as he paints with delicate strokes these lives lived under muslin nets and the East as seen out of these nets.

THE ART REVIEW

Art reviews are similar to book reviews in that they assess the worth of a work of art or of an artist. Here is an excerpt from "Tom Mulder: Painting Indians" in *Utah Holiday*, October 18, 1976.

> I stand before a picture in Phillips Art Gallery in Salt Lake City, Utah. Suddenly home (India) is vividly alive. It spreads beyond the canvas and encapsulates me. I can feel the rhythm of the movements, as three women carry brass pots on their heads and can hear the clinking of their anklets. With his view of both cultures, Southwestern American and subcontinental Asian, Mulder feels one could transport a subcontinental village to the American Southwest, take an Indian posture and make of it a Navajo. The American Southwest of these paintings feels curiously like home. The color, the light are essentially the same; and yet the rugweaver is a Navajo. An artist seeing similarities between two types of "Indians"?

THE BIBLIOGRAPHIC ESSAY

A bibliographic essay surveys research in the field and compares and contrasts the usefulness of various sources on a particular subject. Several publications in the humanities publish biblio graphic essays on a yearly basis to inform scholars of the current developments in the field. Here, for example, is a short excerpt from the "Pound and Eliot" chapter of *American Literary Scholarship.*

> This has been a good year for theoretical work on Pound. Martin A. Kayman connects Pound's theory of the image to his theory of money in "Ezra Pound: The Color of His Money" (*Paideuma* 15, ii–iii: 39–52). I find Kayman's argument here interesting but problematic in his unexamined assumption that Pound never changed, that the aesthetics of 1912-14 are the same as the politics of the 1930s. That is explicitly the argument of an unintelligent essay by Robert Lumsden, "Ezra Pound's Imagism" (*Paideuma* 15, ii–iii: 253–64) who argues that Pound

remained an imagist and that there is no significant distinction
between image, vortex, ideoplasty and ideogram.

Note that in a bibliographic essay the author must include
both his or her assessment of the work at hand and the full
citation of the source. This differs from the annotated
bibliography in which, in the annotation or the summary
assessment, you try *not* to interject a personal point of view and
do *not* include the author's name, the work's title, or publication
information within the summary itself.

THE ANNOTATED BIBLIOGRAPHY

Each entry in an annotated bibliography includes the full citation
of a reference source and a short summary or abstract of the
source. The abstract should be a distilled, factual summary;
brevity is important. Try not to include any material from the
citation in the text of the abstract. For example:

> Stead, C. K. *Pound, Yeats, Eliot and the Modernist Movement.* New
> Brunswick: Rutgers University Press, 1986.
>
> Stead's overall theses are as follows: (1) Pound and Eliot
> are central modernists; Yeats is not; and (2) Pound's politics are
> less distasteful than Eliot's because Pound at least had the
> courage of his convictions. The value of the book lies in Stead's
> close readings of many poems by Pound, Eliot, and Yeats. This
> general thrust is to show Eliot's deep influence on Pound in
> matters of form and technique.

CONVENTIONS OF STYLE AND FORMAT

The humanities paper is a single unit in which all the paragraphs
are connected to the thesis and to one another. Although papers
may include internal headings and abstracts, they rarely do so.
Writing in the humanities can be less formal than in the social
sciences and sciences and may be directed at a lay audience.
Note, for example, how much less formal the art review is than
the other examples of common assignments. The book review is
descriptive and evaluative while the bibliographic essay is more
precise. Notice that the entry for the annotated bibliography is

most concise and specific. Clarity and restraint from the overuse of jargon are important considerations. Writing in the first person is acceptable when you are expressing your own reactions and convictions. In other cases, however, you should use an objective tone and write in the third person (he, she, it).

In writing papers for literature, certain conventions of literary analysis are required. You may need to analyze the way a work is constructed. For example: Is it a novel that relies heavily on flashbacks? How does that structure affect the author's purpose or theme? As points of entry into literary analysis you can look at subjects like plot, characterization, theme, the use of imagery, and the writer's style. Literary analysis can be formal, historical, psychoanalytical, or economic. Keep in mind that it is not possible to concern yourself with all of these issues in one paper. You need to decide on one approach and one point of view and then develop that point of view in your paper.

DOCUMENTATION FORMATS

As in all other disciplines, most of the subject areas in the humanities use documentation formats particular to the subject. English and modern and classical language scholars use the MLA format; art, history, music and philosophy scholars use *The Chicago Manual of Style*. Researchers in linguistics and languages use the *Handbook of the Linguistics Society of America* and sometimes the APA format used by the social sciences. (See p. 114 for information on the APA style.)

THE MLA FORMAT*

The MLA format is recommended by the Modern Language Association of America, a professional organization of more than 25,000 teachers of English and other languages. It is required by teachers in the humanities at colleges throughout the United States and Canada. This method of documentation has three parts: parenthetical references in the text, a list of works cited, and content notes. Full sample papers illustrating the MLA format begin on pages 69 and 87.

Parenthetical References in the Text

MLA documentation uses references inserted in parentheses within the text and keyed to a list of works cited at the end of the paper. A typical reference consists of the author's last name and a page number.

> The colony's religious and political freedom appealed to many idealists in Europe (Ripley 132).

If you use more than one source by the same author, shorten the title of each work to one or two key words and include the appropriate shortened title in the parenthetical reference.

> Penn emphasized his religious motivation (Kelley, William Penn 116).

If you state the author's name or the title of the work in your sentence, do not include it in the parenthetical reference. Only a page reference is necessary.

> Penn's political motivation is discussed by Joseph P. Kelley in Pennsylvania, The Colonial Years, 1681-1776 (44).

Keep in mind that you punctuate differently with paraphrases and summaries, quotations run in with the text, and quotations that are set off from the text.

---

*MLA documentation format follows the guidelines set in the *MLA Handbook for Writers of Research Papers*, 4th ed. New York: MLA, 1995.

Parenthetical documentation for *paraphrases and summaries* should appear *before* terminal punctuation marks.

```
Penn's writings epitomize seventeenth-century
religious thought (Degler and Curtis 72).
```

Parenthetical documentation for *quotations run in with the text* should appear *after* the quotation marks but *before* the terminal punctuation.

```
As Ross says, "Penn followed his conscience in
all matters" (127).

We must now ask, as Ross does, "Did Penn follow
Quaker dictates in his dealings with Native
Americans" (128)?

According to Williams, "Penn's utopian vision
was informed by his Quaker beliefs . . ." (72).
```

Parenthetical documentation for *quotations that are set off from the text* should appear two spaces *after* the final punctuation.

```
. . . a commonwealth in which all individuals
can follow God's truth and develop according to
God's will.  (Smith 314)
```

Note: Quotations set off from the text take no quotation marks.

Sample References
Parenthetical references are a straightforward and easy way to provide documentation. Here are the forms required in some special situations.

Works by more than one author

```
One group of physicists questioned many of the
assumptions of relativity (Harbeck and Johnson
31).

With the advent of behaviorism, psychology began
a new phase of inquiry (Cowen, Barbo, and Crum
31-34).
```

For works with more than three authors, list the first author followed by *et al.* ("and others") in place of the rest.

```
A number of important discoveries were made off
the coast of Crete in 1960 (Dugan et al. 63).
```

Two or more works by the same author

To cite two or more works by the same author, include the author's last name and a comma; the complete title, if it is brief, or a shortened version; and the page reference. Thus, two novels by Saul Bellow, *Seize the Day* and *Henderson the Rain King,* would be cited (Bellow, Seize the Day 43) and (Bellow, Henderson 89).

Works with a volume and page number

If you list more than one volume of a multivolume work in the Works Cited list, include the appropriate volume and page number, separated by a colon.

```
In 1912 Virginia Stephen married Leonard Woolf,
with whom she founded Hogarth Press (Woolf 1:
17).
```

If you use only one volume of a multivolume work and have included the volume number in the Works Cited list, include just the page number in the parenthetical reference (Woolf 17).

Works without a listed author

For works without a listed author, use a shortened version of the title in the parenthetical reference.

```
Television ratings wars have escalated during
the past ten years ("Leaving the Cellar" 102).
```

A work that is one page long

Omit the page reference if you are citing a one-page article.

```
It is a curious fact that the introduction of
Christianity at the end of the Roman Empire "had
no  effect  on  the  abolition  of  slavery"
("Slavery").
```

Indirect sources
Indicate that material is from an indirect source by using the abbreviation *qtd. in* ("quoted in") as part of the parenthetical reference.

    Wagner said that myth and history stood before
    him "with opposing claims" (qtd. in Winkler 10).

More than one work within a single set of parentheses
You may cite more than one work within a single set of parentheses. Cite each work as you normally would, separating one from another with semicolons.

    The Brooklyn Bridge has been used as a subject
    by many American artists (McCullough 144;
    Tashjian 58).

Whenever possible, present long references as content notes (see page 58).

Two authors with the same last name
When two of the authors you cite in your paper have the same last name, include the initials in your references. For example, references in the same paper to Wilbert Snow's "The Robert Frost I Knew" and C. P. Snow's "The Two Cultures" would be (Snow, W. 37) and (Snow, C. P. 71).

Literary works
In citations of prose works, it is often helpful to include more than just author and page number. For example, the chapter number of a novel enables readers to locate your reference in any edition of the work to which you are referring. In parenthetical references to prose works, begin with the page number, followed by a semicolon, and add any additional information that might be necessary.

    In Moby Dick, Melville refers to a whaling
    expedition funded by Louis XIV of France (151;
    ch. 24).

In parenthetical references to poems, separate the divisions and line numbers with periods. Title of books in the Bible are often abbreviated (Gen. 5.12). In the following citation, the reference is to book 8, line 124 of *The Aeneid.*

```
Virgil describes the ships as cleaving the
"green woods reflected in the calm water" (The
Aeneid 8.124).
```

An entire work

When citing an entire work rather than part of a work, include just the author's last name in the text of your paper. If you wish, you may mention the author's name in a parenthetical reference.

```
Northrup Frye's Fearful Symmetry presents a
complex critical interpretation of Blake's
poetry.
```

```
Fearful Symmetry presents a complex critical
interpretation of Blake's poetry (Frye).
```

Tables and illustrations

When citing tables and illustrations, include the documentation below the illustrative material.

```
Miscues which alter meaning          51%
Overall loss of comprehension        40%
Retelling score                      20%

Source: Alice S. Horning, "The Trouble with
Writing Is the Trouble with Reading," Journal of
Basic Writing 6 (1987): 46.
```

The List of Works Cited

Your parenthetical references are keyed to a *Works Cited* section that lists all the books, articles, interviews, letters, films, and other sources that you use in your paper. If your instructor wants you to include all the sources you consulted, whether you actually cite them or not, use the title *Works Consulted.*

Arrangement of Citations

Your *Works Cited* section should begin on a new, numbered page after your last page of text. For example, if the text of your paper ends on page 7, then your *Works Cited* list will begin on page 8. The heading *Works Cited* should be centered one inch from the top of the paper. Double-space and begin each entry flush with the left-hand margin. Subsequent lines of the entry should be indented one-half inch (or five spaces if you are using a typewriter) from the left-hand margin. Double-space within and between entries.

In general, entries are arranged alphabetically, according to the last name of each author or to the first word of the title if the author is not known. Articles—*a, an*, and *the*—at the beginning of a title are not considered first words.

Capitalize the first words, last words, and all important words of the title. Do not capitalize articles, prepositions introducing phrases, coordinating conjunctions, and the *to* of infinitives (unless such words are the first or last words of the title). To conserve space, use a shortened form of the publisher's name, and do not include words such as *Incorporated, Company,* or *Publishers* after the name of the publisher. Thus *Holt, Rinehart and Winston* and *Oxford University Press, Inc.* become *Holt* and *Oxford UP*. When a publisher lists offices in several cities, give only the first; for cities outside the United States, add the abbreviation for the country if the city would be ambiguous or unfamiliar to readers (Birmingham, Eng., for example).

Sample Citations: Books

If you are citing books, your entries will contain this information:

1. The author's name (last name first), followed by a period and one space.

2. The title, underlined and followed by a period and one space.

3. The city of publication, followed by a colon.

4. The shortened name of the publisher, followed by a comma.

5. The year of publication, followed by a period.

Notice that an entry has three main divisions separated from one another by a period and one space:

author (last name first)   *title*   *publication information*
            ↓   ↓   ↓
Barsan, Richard Meran. <u>Non-Fiction Film</u>. New York:
Dutton, 1973.

Note: The 1995 MLA Handbook shows one space between main divisions but permits students to use two spaces if their instructor prefers this form.

The following examples illustrate some special situations in which you must vary this basic format.*

A book by one author

Zagorin, Perez. <u>The Court and the Country: The
    Beginning of the English Revolution</u>. New
    York: Atheneum, 1970.

When citing an edition other than the first, indicate the edition number in the form used on the work's title page.

Lawrence, William W. <u>Shakespeare's Problem
    Comedies</u>. 2nd ed. New York: Ungar, 1960.

If the book you are citing contains a title enclosed in quotation marks, keep the quotation marks. If the book contains an underlined title, however, do not underline it in your citation.

Herzog, Alan. <u>Twentieth Century Interpretations
    of "To a Skylark.</u>" Englewood Cliffs:
    Prentice, 1975.

Knoll, Robert E., ed. <u>Storm Over The Waste Land</u>.
    Chicago: Scott, 1964.

A book by two or three authors
Only the first author's name is entered in reverse order; names of the second and third authors appear in normal order. Enter

---

*MLA requires double-spacing within and between citations. Single-spacing has been used in the following examples to save space.

the names in the order in which they appear on the title page.
State each name in full even if two authors have the same last
name.

> Feldman, Burton, and Robert D. Richardson. <u>The</u>
>   <u>Rise of Modern Mythology</u>. Bloomington:
>   Indiana UP, 1972.

A book by more than three authors

For books with more than three authors, list only the first author
followed by *et al.* (and others).

> Prinz, Martin, et al. <u>Guide to Rocks and</u>
>   <u>Minerals</u>. New York: Simon, 1978.

Two or more books by the same author

When listing two books by the same author, include the name in
the first entry, but substitute three unspaced hyphens followed
by a period in subsequent entries. Entries should be arranged
alphabetically according to title.

> Kingston, Maxine Hong. <u>China Man</u>. New York:
>   Knopf, 1980.
> ---. <u>The Woman Warrior</u>. New York: Vintage,
>   1977.

A multivolume work

If you use one volume of a multiple volume work, give the
volume number and the total number of volumes, even if your
paper refers to only one volume.

> Brown, T. Allston. <u>A History of the New York</u>
>   <u>Stage</u>. Vol. 2. New York: Blom, 1903. 2 vols.

A multivolume work in which each volume has an individual title

> Durant, Will. <u>The Renaissance</u>. New York: Simon,
>   1953. Vol. 5 of <u>The Story of Civilization</u>.
>   11 vols. 1935-75.

An edited book
When listing an edited book, begin with the author if you refer mainly to the text itself.

```
Melville, Herman. Moby-Dick. Ed. Charles Fiedel-
    son, Jr. Indianapolis: Bobbs, 1964.
```

If the citations in your paper refer to the work of the editor—the introduction, the editor's notes, or the editor's decisions in editing the text—put his or her name before the title.

```
Fiedelson, Charles, Jr. ed. Moby-Dick. By Herman
    Melville. Indianapolis: Bobbs, 1964.
```

An essay appearing in an anthology
When your paper refers to a single essay in a collection of essays, list the author of the essay first and include all the pages on which the full essay appears, even if you cite only one page in your paper.

```
Forster, E. M. "Flat and Round Characters."
    Theory of the Novel. Ed. Philip Stevick.
    New York: Free, 1980. 223-31.
```

If the essay you cite has been published previously, include publishing data for the first publication followed by the current information along with the abbreviation *Rpt. in* (Reprinted in).

```
Ong, Walter J. "Literacy and Orality in Our
    Times." ADE Bulletin 58 (1978): 1-7. Rpt.
    in Composition and Literature: Bridging the
    Gap. Ed. Winifred Bryan Horner. Chicago: U
    of Chicago P, 1983. 126-40.
```

A cross-reference
If you use more than one essay from a collection, list each essay separately, followed by a cross-reference to the entire collection. In addition, list complete publication information for the collection itself.

```
Bolgar, R. R. "The Greek Legacy." Finley 429-72.
```

Davies, A. M. "Lyric and Other Poetry." Finley
    93-119.
Finley, M. I., ed. The Legacy of Greece. New
    York: Oxford UP, 1981.

An introduction, preface, foreword, or afterword of a book

Beauvoir, Simone de. Preface. Treblinka. By
    Jean-Francois Steiner. New York: Mentor,
    1979. xiii-xxii.

A translation

Carpentier, Alejo. Reasons of State. Trans.
    Francis Partridge. New York: Norton, 1976.

An unsigned article in an encyclopedia

List an unsigned article the way it is cited in the encyclopedia.
Because encyclopedia articles are arranged alphabetically, you
may omit the volume and page numbers when citing one. You
do not have to include publication information for well-known
reference books.

"Liberty, Statue of." Encyclopaedia Britannica:
    Macropaedia. 1985.

A signed article in an encyclopedia

Cite a signed article by stating the author's last name first,
followed by the article's title. When presenting reference books
that are not very well known, present full publication information.

Grimstead, David. "Fuller, Margaret Sarah."
    Encyclopedia of American Biography. Ed.
    John A. Garraty. New York: Harper, 1974.

A reprint of an older edition

When citing a reprint of an older edition—a paperback edition
of a hardback book, for example—give the original publication
date and then the date of the reprint.

Greenberg, Daniel S. <u>The Politics of Pure
Science</u>. 1967. New York: NAL, 1971.

A pamphlet

<u>Existing Light Photography</u>. Rochester: Kodak,
1989.

A government publication

If no author is listed, treat the government agency as the author
of the publication. Give the name of the government followed by
the name of the agency. Underline the title and include the
publishing information that appears on the title page of the
document.

United States. Dept. of State. <u>International
Control of Atomic Energy: Growth of a
Policy</u>. Washington: GPO, 1946.

A short story in an anthology

Faulkner, William. "A Rose for Emily." <u>To Read
Literature</u>. Ed. Donald Hall. 2nd ed. New
York: Holt, 1987. 4-10.

A short story in a collection

Stafford, Jean. "The Echo and the Nemesis."
<u>The Collected Stories</u>. New York: Farrar,
1970. 35-53.

A short poem in a collection

Enclose the title of a short poem in quotation marks.

Pound, Ezra. "A Virginal." <u>Selected Poems
of Ezra Pound</u>. New York: New Directions,
1957. 23.

A book-length poem
Underline the title of a book-length poem.

> Eliot T. S. <u>The Waste Land</u>. <u>T. S. Eliot:</u>
> <u>Collected Poems 1909-1962</u>. New York:
> Harcourt, 1963. 51-70.

A play in an anthology

> Shakespeare, William. <u>Othello, The Moor of</u>
> <u>Venice</u>. <u>Shakespeare: Six Plays and the</u>
> <u>Sonnets</u>. Ed. Thomas Marc Parrott and
> Edward Hubler. New York: Scribner's,
> 1956.

Sample Citations: Articles
In general, a citation for a periodical article contains the following information:

1. The author's name (last name first) followed by a period and one space.*

2. The title of the article, enclosed within quotation marks, followed by a period and one space.*

3. The underlined title of the magazine or journal.

4. The volume number.

5. The date of publication, enclosed within parentheses, followed by a colon.

6. The inclusive pagination of the full article followed by a period.

However, when an article does not appear on consecutive pages—that is, it begins on page 30, skips to page 32, and ends on page 45—include only the first page of the article followed by a plus sign (30+ in this case).
   The following examples illustrate variations on this format.

---

* You may use two spaces after the period if your instructor prefers.

An article in a scholarly journal with continuous pagination through an annual volume

A journal has continuous pagination if the pagination runs consecutively from one issue to the next throughout an annual volume (for example, one issue ends on page 252 and the next begins on page 253). In this case, you include the volume number of the journal in your citation.

```
LeGuin, Ursula K. "American Science Fiction
     and the Other." Science Fiction Studies
     2 (1975): 208-10.
```

An article in a scholarly journal with separate pagination in each issue

A citation for an article in a journal that begins with page 1 in each issue should include the volume number, a period, and then the issue number.

```
Farrell, Thomas J. "Developing Literate
     Writing." Basic Writing 2.1 (1978):
     30-51.
```

An article in a weekly or biweekly magazine

To locate an article in a magazine, a reader needs a day, month, and year of publication, not the volume and issue numbers. In your citation, abbreviate all months except for May, June, and July.

```
Cuomo, Mario. "Family Style." New York 12 May
     1986: 84.
```

An unsigned article in a weekly or biweekly magazine

```
Solzhenitsyn: An Artist Becomes an Exile."
     Time 25 Feb. 1974: 34+.
```

An article in a monthly or bimonthly magazine

In a citation for a magazine published monthly or bimonthly, give the month and year, not the volume and issue numbers.

```
Williamson, Ray. "Native Americans Were
    the First Astronomers." Smithsonian
    Oct. 1978: 78-85.
Gaspen, Phyllis. "Indisposed to Medicine: The
    Women's Self-Help Movement." The New
    Physicians May-June 1980: 20-24.
```

An article in a daily newspaper

Give the name of the newspaper as it appears on the first page
of the paper, but omit the article (Washington Post, not The
Washington Post). Give the date the article appeared, the edition,
and the section if each section is numbered separately, and the
page or pages on which the article appears.

```
Boffey, Phillip M. "Security and Science
    Collide on Data Flow." Wall Street
    Journal 24 Jan. 1982, eastern ed.: 20.
"Madman Attacks Alligator." Smithville
    Observer 14 Aug. 1981, late ed.,
    sec. 4: 5+.
```

An editorial

```
Rips, Michael D. "Let's Junk the National
    Anthem." Editorial. New York Times
    5 July 1986, natl. ed.: A23.
```

A review

After a reviewer's name and the title of the review (if it has one),
write Rev. of followed by the work that is reviewed, a comma, the
word by, and the author. If the review has no listed author, begin
with the title of the review. If the review has neither an author
nor a title, begin with Rev. of and use the title of the work that is
reviewed as a guide when you alphabetize the entry.

```
Nilsen, Don L. F. Rev. of American Tongue
    and Cheek: A Populist Guide to Our
    Language, by Jim Quinn. College
    Composition and Communication 37
    (1986): 107-08.
```

A letter to the editor

> Bishop, Jennifer. Letter. <u>Philadelphia Inquirer</u>.
>   10 Dec. 1987: A26.

Sample Citations: Nonprint Sources
Material from a CD-Rom or Other Portable Database
If the material you are citing appears not only in the portable
database (CD-ROM, diskette, or magnetic tape) but also in a
printed version, your citation should include the author of the
material (if given); the title, source, and date of the printed
version; the title of the database; the publication medium; the
name of the vendor (if known); and the electronic publication
date.

> Russo, Michelle Cash. "Recovering from
>   Bibliographic Instruction Blahs." <u>RQ:
>   Reference Quarterly</u> 32 (1992) 178-83.
>   <u>Infotrac: Magazine Index Plus</u>. CD-ROM.
>   Information Access. Dec. 1993.

If the material you are citing appears in the database only,
and has no printed equivalent, include the author (if given); the
title of the work; the title of the product; the publication medium;
and publication information for the product (place, publisher,
date).

> "Ellison, Ralph." <u>Disklit: American Authors</u>.
>   Diskette. Boston: Hall, 1991.

Material from an Online Database
Enter material from an online database just as you would
material from a portable database. Add the number of pages or
paragraphs (if applicable), the name of the computer service or
network, and the date of access.

> Alston, Robert. "The Battle of the Books."
>   <u>Humanist</u> 7.0176 (10 Sept. 1993): 10 pp.
>   Online. Internet. 10 Oct. 1993.

A lecture

Give the name of the lecturer, the title, the location, and the date on which the lecture took place. Include the sponsoring organization if there is one, and supply a descriptive label if the lecture has no title.

```
Abel, Robert. "Communication Theory and
     Film." Communications Colloquium, Dept.
     of Humanities and Communications.
     Drexel U, 20 Oct. 1986.
```

A personal interview

```
Fuller, Buckminster. Personal interview.
     17 Dec. 1980.
Davidowicz, Lucy. Telephone interview.
     7 May 1985.
```

A personal letter/E-mail

```
Walker, Alice. Letter to the author.
     8 June 1986.
Burke, James Lee. E-mail to the authors.
     15 Mar. 1995.
```

A film

Include the name of the film, the director, the distributor, the year, and any other information that you think is important. If you are emphasizing the contribution of any one person—the director, for example—begin with that person's name.

```
Lucas, George, dir. Return of the Jedi.
     Perf. Mark Hamill, Harrison Ford,
     Carrie Fisher, and Billy Dee Williams.
     Twentieth Century Fox, 1983.
```

A videocassette

```
Arthur Miller: The Crucible. Videocassette.
     Dir. William Schiff. Mosaic Group, 1987.
```

A television or radio program
Include the name of the program (underlined), the network, the
local station, the city, and the date of the program. You may also
include other information that you think is important (the
writers, for example). If an individual program in a series has a
title, include it and put it in quotation marks.

> <u>Nothing to Fear: The Legacy of F.D.R.</u> Narr.
> John Hart. NBC. KNBC, Los Angeles.
> 24 Jan. 1982.
> "The Greening of the Forests." <u>Life on Earth</u>.
> Narr. David Attenborough. PBS. WHYY,
> Philadelphia. 26 Jan. 1982.

Content Notes
Content notes—multiple bibliographic citations or other material
that does not fit smoothly into the text—may be used along with
parenthetical documentation and are indicated by a raised
number in the text. The full text of these notes appears on the
first full numbered page, entitled *Notes*, following the last page
of the paper and before the list of works cited.

For multiple citations
Use content notes for references to numerous citations in a single
reference. These references would be listed in the Works Cited
section.

- **In the paper**

> Just as the German and Russian Jews had
> different religious practices, they also
> had different experiences becoming
> Americanized.[1]

- **In the note**

> [1]Glanz 37-38; Howe 72-77; Manners
> 50-52; and Glazer and Moynihan 89-93.

For explanations
Use notes to provide comments or explanations that are needed
to clarify a point in the text.

- **In the paper**

  > According to Robert Kimbrough, from the
  > moment it was published, reviewers saw
  > <u>The Turn of the Screw</u> as one of Henry
  > James's most telling creations (169).[2]

- **In the note**

  > [2]For typical early reactions to <u>The
  > Turn of the Screw</u>, see Phelps 17; Woolf
  > 65-67; and Pattee 206-07.

- **In the paper**

  > In recent years, Gothic novels have
  > achieved great popularity.[3]

- **In the note**

  > [3]Originally, Gothic novels were
  > works written in imitation of medieval
  > romances and relied on ghosts, super-
  > natural occurrences, and terror. They
  > flourished in the late eighteenth and
  > early nineteenth centuries.

THE CHICAGO FORMAT

*The Chicago Manual of Style**[*] uses notes that appear at the bottom
of the page (footnotes) or at the end of the paper (endnotes) and
bibliographic citations at the end of the paper. Indent the first
line of each note and the second and subsequent lines of each
bibliographic citation three spaces. In both notes and bibliography, single-space between the major divisions of each entry.
The notes format uses a raised numeral at the end of the sentence
in which you have either quoted or made reference to an idea or
a piece of information from a source. This same number should
appear at the beginning of the note. The first time you make
reference to a work you use the full citation; *subsequent references
to the same work should list the author's last name,*

---

*The Chicago format follows the guidelines set in *The Chicago Manual of Style*. 14th ed.
Chicago: University of Chicago Press, 1993.

followed by a comma, and a page number. When more than one work by the same author is cited, a short title is necessary.*

- **First note on Espinoza**

      1. J. Manuel. Espinoza, <u>First Expedition</u>
      <u>of Vargas in New Mexico, 1692</u> (Albuquerque:
      University of New Mexico Press, 1940),
      10-15.

- **Bibliographic form**

      Espinoza, J. Manuel. <u>First Expedition of</u>
          <u>Vargas in New Mexico, 1692</u>. Albuquerque:
          University of New Mexico Press, 1940.

- **Subsequent notes on Espinoza**

      2. Espinoza, 69.
      3. Espinoza, 70.

If you are required to use *footnotes,* be sure that the note numbers on a particular page of your paper correspond to the footnotes at the bottom of the page. *Endnotes* are all of your notes on a separate sheet at the end of the paper under the title *Notes.*

Sample Citations for Notes: Books

A book by one author

      1. Herbert J. Gans, <u>The Urban Villagers</u>, 2d
      ed. (New York: Free Press, 1982), 100.

A book by two or three authors

      2. James West Davidson and Mark Hamilton
      Lytle, <u>After the Fact: The Art of Historical</u>
      <u>Detection</u> (New York: Alfred Knopf, 1982), 54.

The Chicago Manual of Style requires double-spacing within and between notes and bibliographic entries. Single-spacing has been used in the following examples to save space.

A multivolume work

3. Kathleen Raine, <u>Blake and Tradition</u>
(Princeton: Princeton University Press,
1968), 1: 100.
4. Will Durant and Ariel Durant, <u>The Age of
Napoleon: A History of European Civilization
from 1789 to 1815</u>, vol. 11, <u>The Story of
Civilization</u> (New York: Simon and Schuster,
1975), 90.

An edited book

5. William Bartram, <u>The Travels of William
Bartram</u>, ed. Mark Van Doren (New York: Dover
Press, 1955), 85.

An essay in an anthology

6. G.E.R. Lloyd, "Science and Mathematics,"
in <u>The Legacy of Greece</u>, ed. M.I. Finley (New
York: Oxford University Press, 1981), 256-300.

An article in an encyclopedia (unsigned/signed)

7. <u>The Focal Encyclopedia of Photography</u>,
1965 ed., s.v. "Daguerreotype."
8. <u>The Encyclopedia of Philosophy</u>, 1967 ed.,
s.v. "Hobbes, Thomas" by R.S. Peters.

The abbreviation *s.v.* stands for *sub verbo*—"under the word."

Sample Citations for Notes—Articles

An article in a scholarly journal with continuous pagination through an annual volume

1. John Huntington, "Science Fiction and
the Future," <u>College English</u> 37 (fall 1975):
340-58.

An article in a scholarly journal with separate pagination in each issue

> 2. R. G. Sipes, "War, Sports, and Aggression: An Empirical Test of Two Rival Theories," <u>American Anthropologist</u> 4, no. 2 (1973): 84.

An article in a weekly magazine

> 3. Sharon Bergley, "Redefining Intelligence," <u>Newsweek</u>, 14 November 1983, 123.
> 4. "Solzhenitsyn: A Candle in the Wind," <u>Time</u>, 23 March 1970, 70.

An article in a monthly magazine

> 5. Lori Roll, "Careers in Engineering," <u>Working Woman</u>, November 1982, 62.

An article in a newspaper

> 6. Raymond Bonner, "A Guatemalan General's Rise to Power," <u>New York Times</u>, 21 July 1982, 3(A).

Sample Citations for Bibliographies: Books

A book by one author

> Gans, Herbert J. <u>The Urban Villagers</u>, 2d ed. New York: Free Press, 1982.

A book by two or more authors

> Davidson, James West, and Mark Hamilton Lytle. <u>After the Fact: The Art of Historical Detection</u>. New York: Alfred Knopf, 1982.

A multivolume work

> Raine, Kathleen. Blake and Tradition. Vol. 1.
> Princeton: Princeton University Press, 1968.
> Durant, Will, and Ariel Durant. The Age of
> Napoleon: A History of European Civilization
> from 1789 to 1815. Vol. 11, The Story of
> Civilization. New York: Simon and Schuster,
> 1975.

An edited book

> Bartram, William. The Travels of William
> Bartram, edited by Mark Van Doren. New
> York: Dover Press, 1955.

An essay in an anthology

> Lloyd, G. E. R. "Science and Mathematics."
> In The Legacy of Greece, edited by M. I.
> Finley, 256-300. New York: Oxford
> University Press, 1981.

An article in an encyclopedia (unsigned/signed)

> The Focal Encyclopedia of Photography. 1965 ed.,
> s.v. "Daguerreotype."
> The Encyclopedia of Philosophy. 1967 ed., s.v.
> "Hobbes, Thomas," by R.S. Peters.

In a bibliography, these works are listed according to the name of the encyclopedia. The abbreviation *s.v.* stands for *sub verbo* ("under the word"). Most encyclopedias are arranged alphabetically according to key terms. Providing the key word allows your reader to find the appropriate entry.

Sample Citations for Bibliographies: Articles

An article in a scholarly journal with continuous pagination through an annual volume

> Huntington, John. "Science Fiction and the
> Future." <u>College English</u> 37 (fall 1975):
> 340-58.

An article in a scholarly journal with separate pagination in each issue

> Sipes, R. G. "War, Sports, and Aggression: An
> Empirical Test of Two Rival Theories."
> <u>American Anthropologist</u> 4, no. 2 (1973):
> 65-84.

An article in a weekly magazine

> Bergley, Sharon. "Redefining Intelligence."
> <u>Newsweek</u>, 14 November 1983, 123.
> "Solzhenitsyn: A Candle in the Wind." <u>Time</u>, 23
> March 1970, 70.

An article in a monthly magazine

> Roll, Lori. "Careers in Engineering." <u>Working</u>
> <u>Woman</u>, November 1982, 62.

An article in a newspaper

> Bonner, Raymond. "A Guatemalan General's Rise
> to Power." <u>New York Times</u>, 21 July 1982,
> 3(A).

OTHER HUMANITIES FORMATS

Your instructor may require a format other than MLA or Chicago style. Most style manuals are readily available in the reference sections of libraries. *A Manual for Writers of Term Papers, Theses, and Dissertations* by Kate L. Turabian (The University of Chicago Press, 1973) and *Writing About Music: A Style Book for Reports and Theses* by Demar B. Irvine (The University of Washington Press, 1968) are two style manuals that use formats based on the Chicago style.

SAMPLE HUMANITIES PAPERS

The following papers illustrate the MLA and Chicago styles of documentation. The first two papers—"The Italian Family: 'Stronghold in a Hostile Land'" and "Rudolfo Anaya's *Bless Me, Ultima*: A Microcosmic Representation of Chicano Literature"— use the MLA format. The third paper, "Anglo-American Policy in the Caribbean," follows the Chicago format.

SAMPLE HUMANITIES PAPER:
MLA FORMAT
[No title page; with outline]

Michael Schrader
Dr. Patterson
English 102
April 18, 1989

1" from top of page

                    The Italian Family:
                "Stronghold in a Hostile Land"

Thesis Statement: Although emigration from Italy
led to assimilation, which weakened the family
system to some extent, the Italian family in the
United States remains unusually close and
stable.

double-space through-out

I. Most Italian immigrants came to America
   from the Mezzogiorno.
   A. In Italy, each village was separate
      and unique.
      1. Each village had its own customs.
      2. Villagers identified with
         family and village.
   B. In America, Italians recreated their
      Italian villages.
      1. Italians in America established
         customs and living conditions
         like those in Italy.
      2. In America, Italians began to
         identify with other Italians.
II. Most Italians from the Mezzogiorno were
    of the contandini or giornalieri classes,
    which relied heavily on the extended
    family.
    A. The southern Italian family was
       usually patriarchal.
       1. The mother maintained the home
          and managed the finances.

sentence outline of student's paper

2. The father earned the money
   and made all major decisions.

B. Children's roles mirrored adult
   roles.

1. Parents prepared their sons
   to be heads of households.

2. Parents prepared their
   daughters to love and obey
   their husbands.

III. Family solidarity insulated the <u>contadino</u>
family from the hostile outside world.

A. Barzini sees the family as a
   "stronghold" and a "refuge."

B. Italians did not trust outsiders.

IV. Italians in America have remained somewhat
aloof.

A. Immigrants often joined fellow
   villagers in urban "Little Italys."

1. Most Italians remain in
   northeastern United States.

2. Italians are more likely to
   improve old neighborhoods
   than to relocate.

3. Two generations often move
   to suburbs together.

4. Italians are more likely to live
   near parents and siblings than
   other ethnic groups.

B. Immigrants maintain a family-
   oriented society in America.

V. The Italian family in America has under-
gone many changes.

A. Some women have sought employment.

Schrader iii

B. Conflicts have occurred between
   parents and children.
C. The family system has changed.
   1. The family has become less
      patriarchal and more democratic.
   2. Third-generation Italian-Americans
      have relaxed the rigid sex roles
      of Old World society to some
      extent.
   3. Third-generation Italian-Americans
      often prefer to associate with
      friends rather than relatives.
VI. Despite changes, the family remains close
    and stable.
A. The Italian family remains close.
   1. The extended family has become
      more important.
   2. Italians are more likely than
      other ethnic groups to open their
      homes to elderly relatives.
   3. The family provides emotional and
      social support.
B. The Italian family remains stable.
   1. Italians have low rates of divorce,
      separation, and desertion.
   2. Italians have a low intermarriage
      rate.

Schrader 1

1/2" from top of page

The Italian Family:
"Stronghold in a Hostile Land"

centered title

Most of the Italian immigrants who came to America between 1900 and 1930 were from Southern Italy. They came from small villages where they had been peasant farmers, peasant workers, or artisans. When they emigrated to America, these southern Italians brought with them their close family system and their enormous respect for the family unit. Even with all of the demands and pressures of adjusting to life in a foreign country, the family remained the number-one priority for the Italians. Today, this is still true among Italian-Americans. Some assimilation did occur after migration, but it did not take place to the same degree as it did with other ethnic groups. Although emigration from Italy led to assimilation, which weakened the family system to some extent, the Italian family in the United States remains unusually close and stable.

Indent first line of each paragraph one-half inch (five spaces)

background established

The southern peasant Italians came to America from a region known as the Mezzogiorno, which consisted of six provinces south and east of Rome. Each village in this region was self-contained, with its own local church and bell tower, and the language manners, and mores differed from village to village. Francis Femminella and Jill Quadagno note that in Italy, the people did not see themselves as Italians; instead they identified with their families, villages, and towns. When the Italian villagers migrated to America, they naturally sought out their <u>paisani</u>, their fellow villagers, who had

introduces material from source

Schrader 2

already come to the United States. There they
tried to establish customs and living conditions
similar to those they had left behind. In fact,
Italian immigrants did not really take on an
Italian ethnic identity until after they arrived
in America (61-64).

*last name
and page
number
on every
page*

As Herbert Gans notes, most southern
Italians belonged to the peasant class of
farmers called the contadini or to the class of
day laborers known as giornalieri. Both these
groups were very poor (199-200). Femminella and
Quadagno believe that it was because of this
poverty, and because they were exploited by
landowners, that these classes rejected the
social institutions of the rest of the country
and came to rely almost exclusively on the
family (65). For the southern Italian, however,
family meant not only husband, wife, and
children, but also grand-parents, uncles, aunts,
and cousins--in fact, all blood relatives--and
even godparents.

*transi-
tional
paragraph*

According to Femminella and Quadagno, the
southern Italian family is usually seen as
patriarchal, but although the father was the
head of the family, the mother had a great deal
of power. For example, the mother was
responsible for maintaining the home, the true
center of the family; for arranging her
children's marriages; and for managing financial
affairs. The father made all major decisions
that involved the family's relationship with the
world at large and, of course, was responsible
for earning a living (65-66). In short, as
Virginia Yans-McLaughlin points out, the Italian

*summary
of two
pages of
source
material*

family was "father-dominated but mother-centered" (84).

> quotation marks around a short quotation

Children were a very important part of the family, and the roles defined for them by their parents mirrored traditional adult roles. For instance, Patrick Gallo observes that although parents of the peasant class wanted their children to be well educated in proper behavior, their expectations were very different for their sons and their daughters. Male children were taught to be patient, to have inner control over their emotions, and to show respect for their elders and acknowledge their wisdom. The females were taught household skills and encouraged to develop qualities that would enable them to take their place as the center of the family (Old Bread 152).

> paraphrase of source material

Family solidarity gave the southern Italians a sense of unity and cohesiveness (Gallo, Old Bread 152). Within the family, a strong value system protected each individual from a hostile environment. Luigi Barzini describes the role of the family in Italian society in this way:

> The Italian family is a stronghold in a hostile land; within its walls and among its members, the individual finds consolation, help, advice, provision, loans, weapons, allies, and accomplices to aid in his pursuits. No Italian who has a family is ever alone. He finds in it a refuge in which to lick his wounds after a defeat, or an arsenal and a staff for

> quotation of more than four lines indented one inch (10 spaces) from left margin

Schrader 4

his victorious drives. (qtd. in
Gallo, <u>Old Bread</u> 152)

indirect quotation

The Italian family was so strongly bonded that
it became the most powerful single unit to the
individual. Since Southern Italy was perceived
as threatening and lawless, the family was the
only unit the individual could rely on.

The southern Italian family rarely became
entangled in conflicts outside its own close-
knit unit. If individuals placed any type of
trust outside the family, they were considered
by members of their own family to be taking
risks that in the end could cause them to lose
everything. To go outside the family for help
was just not done since by so doing Italians
would be placing themselves in a situation where
"the form was alien, the access unequal, the
rules unknown, and the justice pernicious"
(Gallo, <u>Old Bread</u> 156).

As Yans-McLaughlin points out, the Italians
came to America with a culture that was in many

transitional paragraph

ways different from a rapidly developing industrial society, a society that needed their labor
but rejected their "unusual" customs. The extent
to which they were successful in staying apart
from the larger society can be seen through an
examination of the characteristics of Italian-
Americans today. Although assimilation has
occurred, cultural traditions, maintained by
strong family ties, have affected the relationship of the Italians to American society (79).
In addition, Yancy, Ericksen, and Juliani
believe that the Italians have become increasingly aware that their ethnic identity has been

maintained by the stability and isolation of
their communities and by their reliance on the
services and institutions offered by their
communities (399).

　　Many Italian families migrated to America
to join relatives or friends from their
villages. At the beginning of the immigration,
many Italians settled into areas known as
"Little Italys," urban neighborhoods "where
relatives often lived side by side, and in the
midst of people from the same Italian town.
Under these conditions, the family circle was
maintained much as it had existed in Southern
Italy" (Gans 205). To a great extent, these
"Little Italys" have been maintained, becoming
extended families for their residents. The 1960
census showed that almost 70 percent of Italian-
Americans were still clustered in the northeastern region of the United States (Femminella
and Quadagno 77). Glazer and Moynihan note that
second- and third-generation Italian-Americans
are more likely to work to improve old neighborhoods than to move. When they do leave old
neighborhoods, children and parents often move
together (187). National Opinion Research Center
surveys have found that Italians are more likely
than other ethnic groups to live in the same
neighborhood as their closest family members and
to visit them regularly (Femminella and Quadagno
77). Italian-Americans also exhibit a strong
sense of loyalty to and responsibility for their
paisani, insisting, for instance, that family
and community should house and support their own
indigents rather than relying on government

*combination
of four
sources by
paraphrasing,
summarizing,
and
quoting*

Schrader 6

agencies (Sons of Italy). It is clear that many
Italian-Americans value their ethnic solidarity
and their independence from the larger society.

summary of paragraph's main idea

Italian immigrants have by and large maintained their Old World family system in the
United States. As Yans-McLaughlin observes, the
type of society they left behind is frequently
referred to as "familistic" because the individual's social role was defined primarily by the
family (61). In the United States as in Italy,
the importance of the family over the community
or the individual was maintained, and this too
kept Italians somewhat aloof from outsiders.

paraphrase of a source

Despite this cohesiveness, the first-
generation Italian family in Armerica was in
transition. It was torn between the Italian culture transmitted by the family and the American
culture transmitted by American institutions. As
Femminella and Quadagno point out, many changes
occurred when the family came to America. When
the Italian immigrants arrived in America, many
were faced with difficulties in finding work. It
was often necessary for the mother to go out and
find a job. In Southern Italy, the mother rarely
left the house to go out and work, but in America her employment was often necessary for the
family's survival. Some researchers view this as
a breakdown of the Italian-American family, but
others disagree, believing women took only those
jobs that they felt were in line with the family
value system--for instance, work in a factory
that employed other Italian-American women (71).
Father Vincent P. D'Ancona, a parish priest in
the heavily Italian South Philadelphia area,

transitional sentence

combination of two print sources and two inter-views by paraphrase and direct quotation

reports that even today a wife's or mother's
need to seek employment remains one of the primary sources of family tension, whether the need
is economic or emotional. Conflicts also occurred among parents and their children--even
though many children agreed that their parents
were "too good to fight with" (Gallo, <u>Old Bread</u>
159). Both Father D'Ancona and barber Anthony
Pesca, long-time residents of South Philadelphia, observe that today parents and children
(despite their love and respect for each other)
regularly engage in heated quarrels over issues
like dating and curfews, use of drugs and alcohol, and church attendance. The most sensitive
issue, Father D'Ancona believes, is the desire
of a child to live outside the community or to
marry a non-Italian.[1]

> *reference to content note*

    Although some patterns did remain the same,
the Old World family system changed as time went
on. Paul J. Campisi's often-cited 1948 study,
"Ethnic Family Patterns: The Italian Family in
the United Staes," examines the changes between
the southern Italians and first- and second-
generation Italian-Americans. One of the major
changes this study found was that although the
peasant family was primarily ruled by the
father, by the second generation the family had
become democratic, with the father's position
more equal to that of the mother and children.
Campisi also found that the influence of Italian
culture was growing weaker with more and more
cultural values shaped by the larger society
rather than by the family (443-49). As recently
as 1962, however, Herbert Gans noted that the

> *summary of main points of source*

> *period after page numbers in parentheses*

Schrader 8

husband was still the breadwinner and the
wife's primary responsibilities were still her
home and children. In fact, in Gans's working-
class population, the roles of husband and wife
were clearly differentiated (50-52). But in the
1982 update of his study, when he considers the
third generation of Italian-Americans, Gans
finds that even in Italian urban neighborhoods,
"the traditional social segregation of husbands
and wives has been reduced considerably,
although some men remain reluctant to help with
child-rearing and housework" (231). In his
study, Gans cites an unpublished study of
Bridgeport, Connecticut, by James Crispino. As
Gans notes, Crispino reports that while his
third-generation Italian-Americans felt very
close to their relatives, more and more often
"friends replaced family members as preferred
associates . . . and many were not Italian-
American or peers they had known since
childhood" (230). It is clear, then, that some
aspects of the traditional family systems are
changing.[2]

ellipsis indicates deletion of part of source

Despite these changes, however, the
Italian-American family has remained close-knit
and stable. After coming to America, the
Italian-American family continued to be
extremely close. In fact, in one study, which
involved fifty first-generation and ninety
second-generation Italian-American adults from
an ethnic neighborhood in New York City,
researchers found that the extended family was
more important to second-generation than to
first-generation Italian-Americans.

Schrader 9

Although the second-generation family had generally become larger, relatives tended to live in
closer physical proximity and to have closer and
more extensive social ties with one another
(Palisi 49-50). Today, Italians remain more
likely than members of most other ethnic groups
to have relatives over age sixty living with
them (Goodman). A walking tour of a typical
urban Italian-American neighborhood seems to
support this conclusion, showing a large propor-
tion of elderly residents, often accompanied by
children and grandchildren as they go about
routine errands and shopping. Even when members
of the extended family are not actually part of
the household, the relationships among family
members are close; the family provides emotional
support and also serves as a social network
(Gans 46). In fact, even Italian-American gang-
sters typically maintain very close and highly
stable family relationships (Glazer and Moynihan
196).

    The stability of the Italian family is re-
flected in the low rates of divorce and intermarriage. The 1970 census showed that only about
three percent of all Italian-Americans were di-
vorced and that the divorce rate was not significantly higher for younger Italians. Alfred J.
Tella, special advisor to the Director of the
Census Bureau, notes that despite increasing
affluence, Italian-Americans retain closer
family ties than other groups. Tella sees the
fact that Italians as a group get fewer divorces
as one indication of this continued closeness
(Goodman). Glazer and Moynihan support this

*no page
number
when
source
is one
page long*

Schrader 10

view. They say: "That the family is 'strong' is
clear. Divorce, separation, and desertion are
relatively rare. Family life is considered the
norm for everyone. . . ."(197). Moreover, two
separate studies show Italians to have one of
the lowest intermarriage rates; therefore, it
can be concluded that they retain a high degree
of ethnic identity (Femminella and Quadagno 74).

Several conclusions may be drawn about the
Italian-American family today. Assimilation has
occurred, but the notion of the importance of   *conclusion*
family has been passed down from generation to
generation and has remained an important
characteristic of the Italian-American family.
As Frank Mucci, a third-generation Italian-American says, "You can't do without your family,
and they can't do without you. Your family has
to stay your first responsibility, no matter
what happens." So far, the stable Italian family   *direct*
system has survived through the years, and it   *quotations*
                                                     from
seems likely to continue to do so. As Patrick   *personal*
Gallo notes, "The family for the southern   *letter*
Italian remains the supreme societal
organization" (Ethnic 87).

Schrader 11

Notes

[1] Because of the many interruptions in the interview with Mr. Pesca, I was unable to determine which issue he views as most likely to produce serious conflict between parents and children.

[2] The nomination of Congresswoman Geraldine Ferraro, an Italian-American wife and mother, as the Democratic vice-presidential candidate in 1984 seems to support the impression that the role of women in the Italian family is changing.

content notes provide supplementary information

Schrader 12

Works Cited

Campisi, Paul J. "Ethnic Family Patterns: The
Italian Family in the United States."
American Journal of Sociology 53 (1948):
443-49.

D'Ancona, Father Vincent P. Personal interview.
10 Feb. 1989.

Femminella, Francis X., and Jill S. Quadagno.
"The Italian-American Family." Ethnic
Families in America. Ed. Charles H. Mindel
and Robert W. Habenstein. New York:
Elsevier, 1976. 61-88.

Gallo, Patrick J. Ethnic Alienation. Cranbury:
Fairleigh Dickinson UP, 1974.

---. Old Bread, New Wine. Chicago: Nelson-Hall,
1981.

Gans, Herbert J. The Urban Villagers. 2nd ed.
New York: Free, 1982.

Glazer, Nathan, and Daniel Patrick Moynihan.
Beyond the Melting Pot. 2nd ed. Cambridge,
Mass.: MIT P, 1970.

Goodman, Walter. "Scholars Find Bad Image Still
Plagues U.S. Italians." New York Times 15
Oct. 1903, late ed.: B25.

Mucci, Frank. Letter to author's grandmother. 17
Nov. 1980.

Palisi, Bartolomeo S. "Ethnic Generation and
Family Structure." Journal of Marriage and
Family 28 (1966): 49-50.

Pesca, Anthony. Telephone interview. 10 Feb.
1989.

Sons of Italy Meeting. Philadelphia, Pa. 30
March 1989.

Indent second and subsequent lines of each entry one-half inch (five spaces)

all material double-spaced

three hyphens to indicate same author as above

cites volume, year, pages

Schrader 13

Walking Tour. South Philadelphia. 10 Feb. 1989.
Yancy, William L., Eugene Ericksen, and Richard
    N. Juliani. "Emergent Ethnicity: A Review
    and Reformulation." American Sociological
    Review 41.3 (1976): 391-403.
Yans-McLaughlin, Virginia. Family and Community:
    Italian Immigrants in Buffalo. Ithaca:
    Cornell UP, 1977.

SAMPLE HUMANITIES PAPER: MLA FORMAT
[With title page; no outline]

Rudolfo Anaya's <u>Bless Me, Ultima:</u>

A Microcosmic Representation of Chicano

Literature

by

Jennifer Flemming

English 3112

Dr. Jussawalla

May 12, 1986

Rudolfo Anaya's <u>Bless Me, Ultima</u>: A
Microcosmic Representation of Chicano Literature

Chicano authors have sometimes been called
"noble savages" and they have been denied credit
and recognition in the field of literature and
culture. Some scholars and teachers consider
Chicano literature as "newly emerged" from
recent political developments and therefore
lacking in maturity and universal appeal, although others have traced its growth and development in the Southwest since the sixteenth
century. The fact that most Chicano literature
is based on social protest and is associated
with political events also elicits less than
positive responses from literary critics. The
political nature of the literature causes it to
be viewed as not quite legitimate. However,
Chicano literature is neither "newly emerged"
and thus lacking in maturity, nor merely reflec-
tive of recent socio-political movements. On the
contrary, Chicano literature--writing done by
American Hispanics--not only records the Mexican-American experience in the American Southwest but also demonstrates the universality of
that experience. Rudolfo Anaya's <u>Bless Me,
Ultima</u>, which records the Mexican-American
experience while describing the emotions universal to most 10-year-old boys, exemplifies the
dual role of the best Chicano literature.

Paredes and Paredes's definition of Chicano
literature ties it to the Chicano's key role in
the cultural development of the American
Southwest:

People like to record their experiences; Mexican-Americans have been no
exception. They have had much to write
about. Their lives have sometimes been
stormy and often tragic, but always
vital and intriguing. It is hardly
surprising that Mexican-Americans have
literary talents, for they are heirs
to the European civilization of Spain
and the Indian civilizations of
Mexico, both of which produced great
poets and storytellers. Furthermore,
they have also been in contact with
the history and literature of the
United States.... (1)

This connection of the development of the
literature with the locale is made by Luis Leal
in his article "Mexican American Literature: A
Historical Perspective," when he notes that Chicano literature had its origin when the Southwest was settled by the inhabitants of Mexico
during colonial times (22). He emphasizes that
the literature originated both from the contact
of the colonial Mexicans with the Native Americans and from the contact with the Anglo culture that was moving westward. In fact, many of
the themes of Chicano literature emphasize the
coming in contact of two vastly different
cultures. This is particularly true of Anaya'a
Bless Me, Ultima, which also reflects the universal emotions and feelings generated as a
result of the clash of cultures.

A recording of the experience of the Southwest is found in Anaya's Bless Me, Ultima, which

ultimately relates universal themes of initia-
tion and maturation (Novoa, "Themes"). In his
novel about the rites of passage of a young boy
(Antonio) from innocent adolescence to the
ambiguous and morally corrupt adult world, the
author expresses his culture's indigenous
beliefs, myths, and legends.

Antonio's father tells him of the coming of
the Spanish colonizers to the Valley, their
contact with the American-Indian culture which
Ultima--an older grandmother figure--exempli-
fies, and the changes brought about in the village and the town by the coming of the Tejanos.
Yet the theme is universal, transcending the
boundaries of his village. The events that result from the clash between the old and the new
could take place anywhere in the world because
they deal with religious hatred and with the
conflicts between different ways of life.

The novel relates the story of a young boy
and his friendship with a curandera (shaman)
named Ultima who comes to live with Antonio and
his family. The arrival of Ultima has an
enormous impact on him because he feels a
kinship with her. For instance, through Ultima,
Antonio--now nicknamed Tony--comes in contact
with the local Indian religions. Ultima teaches
him about herbs and their potency in creating
conditions often associated with magic. She also
introduces Antonio to Narcisso, the Indian who
teaches him the myth of the Golden Carp: "The
people who killed the carp of the river . . .
were punished by being turned into fish themselves. After that happened many years later,

a new people came to live in this valley" (Anaya
110). This myth encapsulates the history of the
Indian people, the Hispanic colonizers, and the
Anglo settlers of New Mexico. Tony sees the
reflection of the myth in his day-to-day life.
The Indians and the Hispanics of the valley are
gradually replaced by the "new people," the
Anglos. This stirs in him deep love for his
land, his people, and his lifestyle.

But at school he is teased for believing in
these myths. His classmates, who have already
laughed at his lunch of tortillas and his
inability to speak English, taunt him about
Ultima. Calling her a bruja (witch) they say,
"Hey, Tony, can you make the ball disappear?"
"Hey, Tony, do some magic" (Anaya 102). Tony
suffers the angst of a ten-year-old taunted by
these voices. He begins to suffer doubts about
his identity and the rightness of his beliefs.

At the end of the book, when Ultima is
killed by the townspeople for being a witch,
Antonio falls to his knees to pray for her and
in facing her death reaches his maturation. He
knows what is right for him: "I praised the
beauty of the Golden Carp" (Anaya 244).

Anaya has said, "When people ask me where
my roots are, I look down at my feet. . . . They
are here, in New Mexico, in the Southwest."
(Novoa, Chicano Authors 185). The author's
message is clear and undeniable: One must go
back to one's roots, despite the conflicting
pull of Americanization. It is the same message
of faith and hope, which Ultima, on her

deathbed, gives to Antonio: learn to accept life's
experiences and feel the strength of who you are. In
the character of Ultima, however, Anaya has created
a symbol of beauty, harmony, understanding, and the
power of goodness that transcends the limits of time
and space and religious beliefs.

From the above examples it can be seen that
Anaya is capable of producing Chicano literature
that has universal appeal and themes. Anaya's novel
records the Mexican-American experience of the
Southwest while creating characters and portraying
emotions of universal appeal. The social protest
against Americanization is secondary to the treatment of myth and emotions.

Chicano literature cannot be considered just a
byproduct of the recent struggle for civil rights.
This is not to minimize or deny the effects of the
Chicano political movement and the new sense of
awareness and direction that it has sparked (which
includes the proliferation of Chicano literary
texts). Although Chicano literature may appear to
emphasize social protest and criticism of the
dominant Anglo culture, or seem to be introspec-
tively searching for self-definition, it will not be
found lacking in universal appeal (Leal et al. 42).

Flemming 6

Works Cited

Anaya, Rudolfo. Bless Me, Ultima. Berkeley:
     Tonatiuh, 1972.

Jimenez, Francisco. The Identification and
     Analysis of Chicano Literature. New York:
     Bilingual, 1979.

Leal, Luis, et al. A Decade of Chicano Liter-
     ature. Santa Barbara: La Causa, 1982.

---. "Mexican American Literature: A Historical
     Perspective." Modern Chicano Writers. Eds.
     Joseph Sommers and Tomas Ybarra-Fausto.
     Englewood Cliffs: Prentice, 1979. 18-40.

Martinez, Julio A., and Francisco A. Lomeli.
     Chicano Literature: A Reference Guide.
     Westport: Greenwood, 1985.

Novoa, Juan-Bruce. "Themes in Rudolfo Anaya's
     Work." Talk given at New Mexico State
     University. Las Cruces, 11 Apr. 1987.

---. Chicano Authors: Inquiry by Interview.
     Austin: U of Texas P, 1980.

Paredes, Americo, and Raymond Paredes. Mexican-
     American Authors. Boston: Houghton, 1973.

SAMPLE HUMANITIES PAPER: CHICAGO FORMAT

Anglo-American Policy in the Caribbean

Thomas C. Howard

History Department

February 1989

Howard 1

Anglo-American Policy in the Caribbean

The formal colonial empire of Britain in
the Caribbean long rested near the informal
American imperial presence. Eventually the
British flag was lowered here as well, suc-
cumbing to nationalistic demands, metropolitan
weariness, and, as emphasized here, international realities. Britain's role in the region
diminished. In relinquishing control, Britain
became here, as elsewhere in the world, the
frequently ambivalent junior partner in what
seemed to be the emerging American world system.
Here, however, she could at least cushion the
trauma of decline with illusions about the
strength and durability of her "special relationship" with her former colonies. Even so,
American anti-colonialism can be seen as a force
in the break-up of the British West Indian
Empire after 1945.

Historically the British West Indian
colonies represented remnants of the Old Empire.
In the mercantilist system of the seventeenth
and eighteenth centuries, they had indeed been
most valuable. The economics of sugar and aboli-
tionism and the needs of the Victorian free
trade empire all left the British West Indies in
a state of neglect for many years and held back
political development. Neglect in the West
Indies, however, was widespread. Despite various
calls for corrective action, little was done
until the 1930s and then only in reaction to a
number of serious civil disturbances and strikes
stemming from the economic dislocations of the
depression. Britain was able to carry on this

policy of benign neglect for so long largely
because of the hemispheric dominance of the
United States, a reality formally acknowledged
in 1902 with the Hay-Pauncefote Treaties,[1] which
solidified regional understanding with the
United States.

In the years after the first World War,
policymakers suspected more and more that the
empire might be "made of porcelain."[2] Cracks did
begin to appear despite efforts to use diplo-
macy, influence, and economics to maintain the
status quo. In 1941 these neglected islands
served as bases for the United States and thus
started the wartime partnership which tempor-
arily revived the entire empire.

It was a unique situation. Here suddenly were
colonies within colonies--American bases, air
strips, and service facilities being constructed
on British colonial soil, all with vast potential for friction and the spread of American
influence. What better place to find examples of
colonial repression to feed the flames of re-
newed American anti-imperialism than right here
in the United States's "own backyard"? What
better place for Britain to attempt to brush up
its colonial image than through development
schemes for the empire? What better place for
emerging nationalist movements to take advantage
of the resurgence of American anti-colonial
sentiments as articulated through the Atlantic
Charter and subsequent wartime statements of
principle? In short, the factor of American
anti-imperialism, which was later to influence

events in India, the Middle East, and Africa,
was first tested in the Caribbean.

So serious, in fact, were anxieties in some
quarters in Britain about American encroachments
in the region by January 1942, that Churchill
sent a personal appeal to Roosevelt reminding
him of his promise to make some statement confirming "that there would be no question of
transfer to the United States of the British
West Indian colonies, either under the bases
agreement or otherwise."[3] Although Roosevelt
agreed to such an assurance, Anglo-American
tensions over the future of the region did not
disappear. Largely because of these tensions, in
fact, the Anglo-Caribbean Commission was created
in 1942. Enthusiastically promoted by the Americans and consented to reluctantly on the British
side, this commission acquired unexpected importance, not only as a functioning regional commission, but as a significant factor in wider
Anglo-American colonial discussion both during
and after the war. Certainly it provided a ready
forum for American criticism. This criticism was
in part responsible for a new Colonial Office
resolve for genuine colonial reform and
development, including political reforms which
would lead eventually to self-government. The
needs of the region had been abundantly revealed
by the work of a royal commission in 1938-1939.
The full text of these recommendations, the
Moyne Report, was not revealed until 1945, but
its stark portrayal of West Indian problems
served as the principal wartime moral incentive
leading to the Colonial Development and Welfare

acts of the 1940s and 1950s.[4] The West Indies, therefore, served as a microcosm of developments which later touched the empire as a whole.

In the immediate post-war period, many of the British suspicions behind Churchill's 1942 message seemed well on the way to fulfillment. In the Caribbean, although the United States had kept its pledge not to annex Britain's colonies, the American influence was more evident than ever. Here, in fact, could be found quite early almost all of the ingredients that were to form the global themes of the second half of the century, not the least of which was American imperialism as anti-communism.

Howard 5

Notes

1. David Weigall, <u>Britain and the World,</u>
<u>1815-1986</u> (New York: Oxford University Press,
1987), 107.

2. John Gallagher, "The Decline, Revival, and
Fall of the British Empire," in <u>The Decline,</u>
<u>Revival, and Fall of the British Empire</u>, ed.
Anil Seal (Cambridge: Cambridge University
Press, 1982), 84.

3. Warren F. Kimball, ed., <u>Churchill and</u>
<u>Roosevelt: Their Complete Correspondence</u>
(Princeton: Princeton University Press, 1984),
1:232.

4. Lord Moyne (Chairman), <u>West India: Royal</u>
<u>Commission Report</u> (London: HMSO, 1945).

Bibliography

Gallagher, John. "The Decline, Revival, and Fall of the British Empire." In The Decline, Revival, and Fall of the British Empire, edited by Anil Seal, 60-95. Cambridge: Cambridge University Press, 1982.

Kimball, Warren F., ed. Churchill and Roosevelt: Their Complete Correspondence. Princeton: Princeton University Press, 1984.

Moyne, Lord (Chairman). West India: Royal Commission Report. London: HMSO, 1945.

Weigall, David. Britain and the World, 1815-1986. New York: Oxford University Press, 1987.

WRITING IN THE
SOCIAL SCIENCES

The social sciences include the following subject areas: anthropology, economics, education, political science, psychology, social work, and sociology. Writing in the social sciences differs from writing in the humanities in that its format conforms to the particular objective of the project or research: exploration, description, explanation, or evaluation. Descriptive and explanatory formats are the dominant forms for the presentation of information in psychology, sociology, anthropology, and political science, where they not only describe individual patterns, but also provide explanations of the dynamics of a group, such as a political organization.

RESEARCH SOURCES

Library research is an important component of research in the social sciences. Only after the researcher has developed a sufficient foundation for the study through library research can he or she pursue data collection through interviews, questionnaires, and field observations. Social scientists survey attitudes, record responses, and interview subjects to obtain reliable evidence. Many of their data are numerical, reported in tables and charts. It is essential for social scientists to know how to read and interpret such figures so that they can analyze data and develop conclusions. Much of your library research in social science disciplines will depend on abstracting information from such tables and charts. Therefore, general reference sources like government yearbooks and almanacs may be particularly useful.

SPECIALIZED LIBRARY SOURCES

The following reference sources are useful in a variety of social science disciplines.

ASI Index (American Statistics Institute)
Encyclopedia of Black America
Handbook of North American Indians
Human Resources Abstracts
International Bibliography of the Social Sciences
International Encyclopedia of the Social Sciences
PAIS Public Affairs Information Service
Population Index
Social Sciences Citation Index

The following reference sources are most often used for research in specific disciplines.

Anthropology

Abstracts in Anthropology
Anthropological Index

Business and Economics

Business Periodicals Index

Criminal Justice

Abstracts on Criminology and Penology
Abstracts on Police Science
Criminal Justice Abstracts
Criminal Justice Periodicals Index

Education

Dictionary of Education
Education Index
Encyclopedia of Educational Research

Political Science

ABC Political Science
CIS Index (Congressional Information Service)

Combined Retrospective Index to Journals in Political Science
Encyclopedia of Modern World Politics
Encyclopedia of the Third World
Foreign Affairs Bibliography
Information Services on Latin America
International Political Science Abstracts
United States Political Science Documents
U.S. Serial Set Index

Psychology

Author Index to Psychological Index and Psychological Abstracts
Contemporary Psychology
Cumulative Subject Index to Psychological Abstracts
Encyclopedia of Psychology
Psychological Abstracts

Sociology

Poverty and Human Resources Abstracts
Rural Sociology Abstracts
Sage Family Studies Abstracts
Sociological Abstracts

Government Documents

Government documents are important resources for social scientists. They contain the most complete and up-to-date facts and figures necessary for any social analysis. Varied information—from technical, scientific, and medical information to everyday information on home safety for children—can be found in government documents.

Government documents can be searched through the *Monthly Catalog*, which contains the list of documents published that month together with a subject index. Other indexes include *The Congressional Information Service Index, The American Statistics Index*, and *The Index to U.S. Government Periodicals.*

Newspaper Articles

Newspaper articles are particularly useful sources for researching subjects in political science, history, economics, or social work. Students usually rely on the *New York Times,* which has indexes available both in print and on microfilm. However, for newspaper information from across the country, a handy and useful source is *Newsbank. Newsbank,* like the government's *Monthly Catalog,* provides subject headings under the appropriate government agencies. For instance, articles on child abuse are likely to be listed under Health and Human Services. Older articles will be listed in older *Newsbanks* under Health, Education, and Welfare. Once you find the subject area, *Newsbank* provides a microcard/microfiche number. On that microfiche, you will find articles from around the country on your subject.

SPECIALIZED DATABASES FOR COMPUTER SEARCHES

Many of the print sources cited above have electronic counterparts. Some of the more widely used databases for social science disciplines include *Cendata, Business Periodicals Index, PsycINFO, ERIC, Social Scisearch, Sociological Abstracts, Information Science Abstracts, PAIS International, Population Bibliography, Economic Literature Index, BI/INFORM, Legal Resources Index, Management Contents, Trade and Industry Index,* and *PTS F+S Indexes.*

NON-LIBRARY SOURCES

Interviews, questionnaires, surveys, and observation of the behavior of various groups and individuals are some of the important non-library sources in social science research. Sometimes students conduct these types of research themselves. Sometimes professors provide unpublished results from these types of research that have been conducted by other students, the professor, colleagues of the professor, institutions, agencies, or research contractors. Assignments given by your professor may ask you to use your classmates as subjects for questionnaires. In political science, your teacher may ask you to interview a sample of college students and classify them as conservative, liberal, or radical. You may be asked to poll each group to find out college students' attitudes on nuclear energy, chemical waste disposal, the homeless, and other issues that affect them. If you were writing a paper on educational programs for gifted students, in addition to library research on the issue, you might want to observe two classes—one of gifted students and one of students not participating in the gifted program. You may also want to interview students, teachers, or parents. In psychology and social work, your research may rely on the observations of clients and patients and be written up as a case study (see p. 112).

ASSIGNMENTS IN THE SOCIAL SCIENCES

In many lower level social science courses, writing assignments take the same form as those in the humanities. However, as students progress into more highly specialized courses during the junior and senior years, they may very well receive assignments that require them to use formats used in the profession they plan to enter. Three of these types of writing are discussed here.

PROPOSALS

Proposals, often the first stage of any research project, help to clarify and focus a research project.

In a proposal, your purpose is to persuade the recipient to grant your request. If an agency is to fund a proposed project, you have to sell its members on your idea. This means that you have to learn to put the purpose of your research project up front and support it. In the process, you must strictly adhere to the specifications outlined in the request for proposals issued by the grant-giving agency.

When an agency provides an RFP (Request for Proposals), it is important to follow the guidelines outlined in the RFP carefully and respond to all issues addressed in the RFP. Remember, priorities are given to proposals that focus on target areas identified in the RFP.

When an agency does not provide an RFP, use the following guidelines.

• **Cover Sheet:** State your name, the title of your project, and the name of the person or agency to whom your proposal is being submitted. Providing a short title will help you express your subject concisely. Thinking about the reader of your proposal will help you sharpen your focus. Usually, another line is added on this sheet that states the reason for the submission of the proposal—for example, a request for funding or facilities.

Advantages of the Maquiladora Project

in El Paso

Submitted to

The Committee on U.S.-Mexico Labor Relations

For

Grant to Research the Benefits of Maquiladora

Employment to El Paso

By Laura Talamantes

• **Abstract:** Usually on a separate page, the abstract provides a short summary of your proposal. (See p. 161 for information about writing abstracts.)

• **Statement of Purpose:** Essentially, this is your thesis statement. It states the purpose of your research project—for example, "The Maquiladora Project is an industrial development program that relies on international cooperation with Mexican industries to use Mexican labor while boosting the employment of U.S. white collar workers."

• **Background of the Problem:** This section should explain why someone should spend time and money solving the problem you have identified. It is usually a paragraph that uses comparisons and contrasts with previous research and indicates the need for your specific research.

- **Rationale:** This section, which justifies further the need for your research project, should be as persuasive as you can make it. Why should the problem you have identified be solved? Why should the question you have posed be answered? Why is the solving of this problem and the answering of this question important at this time?

- **Statement of Qualification:** This section shows why you are qualified to carry out the needed research and what special qualities you bring to your work.

- **Literature Review:** This part can be a brief survey of the information you have looked at that justifies the need for your project and shows the uniqueness of your point of view. In a real-world proposal, this survey needs to be fairly complete, as it helps to establish the writer's credibility as a researcher. Many agencies have already paid for an extensive literature review. They may have identified problems from this literature.

- **Research Methods:** This paragraph describes the exact methods you will use in carrying out your research and the materials you will need. It enables the grantors to determine the soundness of your method.

- **Timetable:** Where applicable, the timetable states the time you will need to carry out the project.

- **Budget:** Where applicable, the budget estimates the costs for carrying out the research.

- **Conclusions:** This section restates the importance of your project.

- **Appendix:** This section contains support materials which would not be included in your text.

A proposal is usually sent with a cover letter, called a letter of transmittal, that follows business letter format. It is accompanied by a brief résumé, one that lists only your qualifications for the project. This résumé summarizes your relevant work experience and accomplishments, and it reinforces your qualifications as presented in the statement of qualification.

CASE STUDIES

Case studies are usually informative, describing the problem at hand and presenting solutions or treatments. They all essentially follow the same format: the statement of the problem, the background of the problem, the methods or processes of the solutions, the conclusions arrived at, and suggestions for improvement or future recommendations. Different disciplines make different uses of case studies. In political science, deliberations in policy making and decision making are subject to the case study methodology. Foreign policy negotiations, for instance, are described and written up as case studies. Issue analyses such as "Should government control the media?" can also be written as case studies.

In psychology, social work, and educational psychology or counseling, the case study is an observation of an individual and his or her interaction with a certain agency. Such a case study usually involves describing the behavior of an individual or a group and outlining the steps to be taken in solving the problem that presents itself to the caseworker or researcher.

The case study that examines a problem in a group or in an environmental context follows the same format. Here is the introduction to a case study based on a social work student's assignment to observe one client.

> Mona Freeman, a 14-year-old girl, was brought to the Denver Children's Residential Treatment Center by her 70-year-old, devoutly religious adoptive mother. Both were personable, verbal, and neatly groomed. The presenting problem was seen differently by various members of the client system: Mrs. Freeman described Mona's "several years of behavioral problems," including "lying, stealing and being boy crazy." Mona viewed herself as a "disappointment" and wanted "time to think." She had been expelled from the local Seventh-Day Adventist School for being truant and defiant several months earlier and had been attending public school. The examining psychiatrist diagnosed a conduct disorder but

saw no intellectual, physical, or emotional disabilities. He predicted that Mona probably would not be able to continue to live in "such an extreme disciplinary environment" as the home of Mrs. Freeman because she had lived for the years from seven until twelve with her natural father in Boston, Massachusetts—a fact which was described as a "kidnapping" by Mrs. Freeman. The psychiatrist mentioned some "depression" and attributed it to Mona's inability to fit in her current environment and the loss of life with her father in Boston.

JOURNAL ARTICLES

• **Abstract:** This short summary appears first, but it is written last. (See p. 161.)

• **Literature Review:** This section includes a statement of the problem and summarizes relevant articles. It is funnel shaped in that it reviews many articles in a very brief space and ends with a sharp focus on the problem.

• **Research Methods:** The purpose of this section is to communicate exactly how you went about your research: description of sample, identification of instruments (interviews, observations, case study), itemization and explanation of procedures. This section should be so explicit that another researcher could replicate the study.

• **Findings:** This section communicates results. It clearly describes the answers to questionnaires, any observations, and test results. Frequently, these results are presented in tables or charts.

• **Discussion:** This section discusses the findings and relates the findings to the literature.

CONVENTIONS OF STYLE AND FORMAT

Social science writing tends to use a technical vocabulary. For instance, in the social work case study, the student speaks of "the presenting problem," which is simply the reason the "subject," Mona, was brought to the Denver Children's Facility. Since you are speaking to specialists when you write papers in these disciplines, it is important to use the vocabulary of the field. Also, in describing charts and figures, it is important to use familiar statistical terms, such as *means, percentages, chi squares,* and other terms in the vocabulary of statistical analysis. But it is also important to explain in plain English what those percentages, means, and standard deviations mean in terms of your analysis.

The social science paper format typically uses internal headings (for example, Statement of Problem, Background of Problem, Description of Problem, Solutions, and Conclusion). Unlike the humanities paper, each section of a social science paper is written as a complete entity with a beginning and an end so that it can be read separately, out of context, and still make complete sense. The body of the paper may present charts or figures (graphs, maps, photographs, flow charts) as well as a discussion of those figures. Numerical data, such as statistics, are frequently presented in tabular form.

DOCUMENTATION FORMAT

Documentation format in the social sciences is more uniform than in the humanities or the sciences. The disciplines and journals in the social sciences almost uniformly use the documentation style of the American Psychological Association's *Publication Manual.*

THE APA FORMAT*

APA format, which is used extensively in the social sciences, relies on short references—consisting of the last name of the author and the year of publication—inserted within the text. These references are keyed to an alphabetical list of references that follows the paper.

---

*APA documentation format follows the guidelines set in the *Publication Manual of the American Psychological Association.* 4th ed. Washington, DC: APA, 1994.

Parenthetical References in the Text

One author
The APA format calls for a comma between the name and the
date, whereas MLA format does not.

```
One study of stress in the workplace
(Weisberg, 1985) shows a correlation
between ...
```

You should not include in the parenthetical reference information
that appears in the text.

```
In his study, Weisberg (1983) shows a
correlation ...
```
(author's name in text)

```
In Weisberg's 1983 study of stress in the
workplace ...
```
(author's name and date in text)

Two publications by same author(s), same year
If you cite two or more publications by the same author that
appeared the same year, the first is designated *a*, the second *b*
(e.g., Weisberg, 1983a; Weisberg, 1983b), and so on. These letter
designations also appear in the reference list that follows the text
of your paper.

```
He completed his next study of stress
(Weisberg, 1983b)....
```

A publication by two or more authors
When a work has two authors, both names are cited every time
you refer to it.

```
There is a current and growing concern over
the use of psychological testing in elemen-
tary schools (Albright & Glennon, 1982).
```

If a work has three, four, or five authors, mention all names in
the first reference, and in subsequent references cite the first
author followed by *et al.* and the year (Sparks et al., 1984). When

a work has six or more authors, cite the name of the first author followed by *et al.* and the year in first and subsequent references.

When citing multiple authors in the text of your paper, join the names of the last two with *and* (According to Rosen, Wolfe, and Ziff [1988] . . .). In parenthetical documentation, however, use an ampersand to join multiple authors (Rosen, Wolfe, & Ziff, 1988).

Specific parts of a source
When citing a specific part of a source, you should identify that part in your reference. APA documentation includes abbreviations for the words *page* ("p."), *chapter* ("chap."), and *section* ("sec.").

> These theories have an interesting history (Lee, 1966, p. 53).

Two or more works within the same parenthetical reference
List works by different authors in alphabetical order. Separate items with a semicolon.

> ... among several studies (Barson & Roth, 1985; Rose, 1987; Tedesco, 1982).

List works by the same author in order of date of publication.

> ... among several studies (Weiss & Elliot, 1982, 1984, 1985).

Distinguish works by the same author that appeared in the same year by designating the first *a,* the second *b,* and so on. (*In press* designates a work about to be published.)

> ... among several studies (Hossack, 1985a, 1985b, 1985c, in press).

Quotation
For a quotation, a page number appears in addition to the author's name and the year.

> Because of information about Japanese success,
> the United States has come to realize that
> "Japanese productivity has successfully chal-
> lenged, even humiliated, America in world competi-
> tion" (Bowman, 1984, p. 197).

The page number for a long quotation (40 words or more) also appears in parentheses but follows the period that ends the last sentence.

> As Rehder (1983) points out,
>   Here women receive low wages, little job
>   security, and less opportunity for training
>   or educational development.... (p. 43)

LISTING THE REFERENCES

The list of all the sources cited in your paper falls at the end on a new numbered page with the heading *References.*

Items are arranged in alphabetical order, with the author's last name spelled out in full and initials only for the author's first and second names. Next comes the date of publication, title, and, for journal entries, volume number and pages. For books, the date of publication, city of publication, and publisher are included. Indent the first line of each entry five to seven spaces. Begin subsequent lines at the left margin.* Double space within and between entries.**

- **In the reference list**

Last name   *Initials*   *Date*   *Underlined title (only first word capitalized)*
  ↓   ↓   ↓   ↓

    Morgan, C.T. (1986). <u>Introduction to psychology.</u>
New York: Knopf.
  ↓   ↓
City   *Publisher*

When determining the order of works in the reference list, keep the following guidelines in mind.

---

*The APA recommends this format for all manuscripts submitted for publication. If your instructor prefers, you may instead type the first line of each entry flush with the left margin and indent subsequent lines three spaces.

**Single-spacing has been used in all APA examples to save space.

- Single-author entries precede multiple-author entries that begin with the same name.

```
Field, S. (1987)...
Field, S., & Levitt, M. P. (1984)...
```

- Entries by the same author or authors are arranged according to the year of publication, starting with the earliest date.

```
Ruthenberg, H., & Rubin, R. (1985)...
Ruthenberg, H., & Rubin, R. (1987)...
```

- Entries having the same author and date of publication are arranged alphabetically according to title. They include lowercase letters after the year.

```
Wolk, E. M. (1986a). Analysis...
Wolk, E. M. (1986b). Hormonal...
```

Sample Citations: Books
Capitalize only the first word of the title and the first word of the subtitle of books. Be sure to underline the title and to enclose in parentheses the date, volume number, and edition number. Separate major divisions of each entry with a period and one space.

A book with one author

```
     Maslow, A. H. (1974). Toward a psychology
of being. Princeton: Van Nostrand.
```

A book with more than one author
Notice that both authors are cited with last names first.

```
     Blood, R.O., & Wolf, D. M. (1960).
Husbands and wives: The dynamics of married
living. Glencoe: Free Press.
```

An edited book

> Lewin, K., Lippitt, R., & White, R. K.
> (Eds.). (1985). Social learning and imitation.
> New York: Basic Books.

A work in more than one volume

> Jones, P.R., & Williams, T.C. (Eds).
> (1990-1993). Handbook of therapy (Vols.
> 1-2). Princeton: Princeton University Press.

Note: The parenthetical citation in the text would be (Jones & Williams, 1990-1993).

A later edition

> Boshes, L. D., & Gibbs, F. A. (1972).
> Epilepsy handbook (2nd ed.). Springfield, IL:
> Thomas.

A book with a corporate author

> League of Women Voters of the United States.
> (1969). Local league handbook. Washington, DC:
> Author.

A book review

Place material that describes the form or content of the reference—review, interview, and so on—within brackets.

> Nagel, J. H. (1970). The consumer view of
> advertising in America [Review of Advertising in
> America: The consumer view] Personal Psychology
> 23, 133-134.

A translated book

> Carpentier, A. (1976). Reasons of state.
> (F. Partridge, Trans.). New York: W. W. Norton.

Sample Citations: Articles

Capitalize only the first word of the title and the first word of the subtitle of articles. Do not underline the article or enclose it in quotation marks. Give the journal title in full; underline the title and capitalize all major words. Underline the volume number and include the issue number in parentheses. Give inclusive page numbers. Separate major divisions of each entry with a period and one space.

An article in a scholarly journal with
continuous pagination through an annual volume

```
        Miller, W. (1969). Violent crimes in city
gangs. Journal of Social Issues 27, 581-593.
```

An article in a scholarly journal that has separate pagination
in each issue

```
        Williams, S., & Cohen, L. R. (1984). Child
stress in early learning situations. American
Psychologist, 21 (10), 1-28.
```

An encyclopedia article

```
        Hodge, R. W., & Siegel, P. M. (1968). The
measurement of social class. In D. L. Sills
(Ed.), International Encyclopedia of the Social
Sciences (Vol. 15, pp. 316-324). New York:
Macmillan.
```

A magazine article

Note: Use *p.* or *pp.* when referring to page numbers in magazines or newspapers *without* volume numbers. Omit the abbreviation for page numbers in referring to publications *with* volume numbers.

```
        Miller, G. A. (1984, November). The test:
Alfred Binet's method of identifying subnormal
children. Science, pp. 55-57.
        Hadingham, E. (1994, April). The Mummies of
Xinjiang. Discover, 15 (4), 68-77.
```

A newspaper article

Study finds many street people mentally ill. (1984, June 10). New York Times, p. A7.

Boffy, P. M. (1982, January 24). Security and science collide on data flow. New York Times, p. A20.

An article in an edited book

Tappan, P.W. (1980). Who is a criminal? In M. E. Wolfgang, L. Savitz, & N. Johnston (Eds.), The sociology of crime and delinquency (pp. 41-48). New York: Wiley.

A government publication

National Institute of Mental Health. (1985). Television and the family: A report on the effect on children of violence and family television viewing (DHHS Publication No. ADM 851274). Washington, DC: U.S. Government Printing Office.

An abstract

Pippard, J., & Ellam, L. (1981). Electroconvulsive treatment in Great Britain. British Journal of Psychiatry, 139, 563-568. (From Psychological Abstracts, 1982, 68, Abstract No. 1567)

An interview

Anderson, A., & Southern, T. (1958). [Interview with Nelson Algren]. In M. Cowley (Ed.), Writers at work (pp. 231-249). New York: Viking.

If the interview is not published, it does not appear in "References." Instead, the text of the paper should clarify the interview's nature and date. The same applies to other personal communications, including letters and electronic messages.

Non-print Sources

A film or videotape

```
Kramer, S. (Producer), & Benedek, L.
(Director). (1951). Death of a salesman [Film].
Burbank: Columbia.
```

Electronic media
APA recommends the following generic formats for referring to on-line information:

```
Author, I. (date). Title of article.
Title of Periodical [On-line], xx. Available:
Specific path
Author, I. (date). Title of article.
[CD-ROM]. Title of Journal, xx, xxx-xxx.
Abstract from: Source and retrieval number.
```

SAMPLE PAPERS IN THE SOCIAL SCIENCES

Two student papers follow. The first one, "Student Stress and Attrition," exemplifies the journal article format. The second one, "A Study of the Relationship of Maternal Smoking During Pregnancy to Low Birth Weight Among Infants Born in a Massachusetts South Shore Hospital," exemplifies the research proposal. They both use APA documentation.

SAMPLE
SOCIAL SCIENCE PAPER:
APA FORMAT

Running head: STUDENT STRESS

Student Stress and Attrition

Gloria E. Medrano

University of Texas at El Paso

Student Stress   2

*short title
and number
on every pa;*

Student Stress and Attrition

*title
repeated*

The National Center for Educational Statistics predicts an overall decrease of 7.5% in
student enrollments between 1980 and 1988. This
statistic translates into a decrease in under-
graduate enrollments for four-year institutions
of approximately 17%. This situation, coupled

*interesting
statistic for
introduction*

with present decreases in federal and state
support for higher education, explains why 60%
of the nation's college presidents agree that
enrollment is a major concern (Dusek & Renteria,
1984).

Ecklund and Henderson (1981), in their
national longitudinal study of the high school
class of 1972, documented how 43% of enrolling
college freshmen had at one point or another
dropped out of college. Thirty-four percent
dropped out within their first two years
(Ecklund & Henderson, 1981). The decreasing

*author's
name
omittted
from cita-
tion when
it appears
in sentence*

student populations and high dropout rates are
directly affecting the state of our educational
system. Although there is little that can be
done about the lower numbers of incoming freshmen, something can be done to lessen the problem
of college attrition.

The ideal approach to combatting this
problem is to deal with the group of students
closest in proximity to the university--the
residence hall population. Many of their reasons
for withdrawing from the university are traced
to a fundamental cause: stress. In this case
stress is the psychological phenomenon that
contributes to the high attrition rates of
resident students.

*states
thesis*

Student Stress   3

Statement of the Problem

The on-campus resident student population is very different from other groups of individuals. They cannot be compared to such groups as non-students, non-commuters, and commuters. Aside from such student-related stressors as academics and personal, financial, and emotional problems, on-campus resident students must also contend with adjusting to their new environment, living away from home and in a new community, having a roommate, and being disturbed by the overall noise level in the dormitories.

distinguishes and classifies the group to be studied

Bishop and Snyder (1976) noted grades and money as the major pressures that account for the differences between residents and commuters. Commuters ranked time management next on their list, and residents listed social pressures and concerns about their future as their next most prominent problem. Residents cited peer pressure more often as sources of stress while commuters were more concerned with difficulties of scheduling.

year in parentheses —author's name in text

Background of the Problem

Resident students at the University of Texas at El Paso experience problems which are different and distinct from other major universities. Of the more than 15,000 students attending this university, slightly more than 700 live on campus. This is a relatively small percentage compared to the neighboring campus of New Mexico State University where over 1,500 of the 12,000 students live on campus, as stated by Richard Hanke in a personal communication on December 2, 1984. U.T. El Paso is a commuter

background of the group to be studied

Student Stress   4

campus, which means that between 1 P.M. and 5
P.M. the campus is virtually deserted. Many
other universities, like N.M.S.U., have campus-
oriented communities. The students have many
activities with which to fill their time. As
stated earlier, the social atmosphere is
directly related to student stress levels.
Many of our on-campus residents are from out of
town, with no means of transportation to get
them off campus, and there is no immediate
community around the campus. They are therefore
unable to expand their social outlets. Another
factor which relates to UTEP is that many of our
residents are freshmen; they are often unfamiliar with many campus activities that would serve
to break the monotony of campus living. Because
of the low numbers of on-campus residents and
the high numbers of commuting students, residents are also limited in terms of the potential
number of people they can interact with.

> *use of comparison and contrast to highlight the problem*

     The new system of incorporating athletes
into the regular student housing system has been
particularly traumatic for non-athlete residents. Previously, athletes were housed in a
separate dormitory, Burges Hall; however, because that hall has fallen into disrepair, the
incoming freshmen football players have been
moved into Barry Hall's third floor. This floor
is between two other non-academic floors. A
non-academic floor is one that is not especially
designated for honors students or other students
requiring special study hours. As such, non-
academic floors do not have designated quiet
hours or rules and regulations that foster

Student Stress   5

study and quiet. Aside from the usual noise
related to living in a non-academic dormitory,
additional problems, such as the dropping of
weights on the floor and disciplinary problems
related to the rowdiness of athletes in general,
also occur.

Description of the Problem

At the beginning of the fall semester of
1984, Barry Hall's second floor had twenty-two
residents. Three residents dropped out of school
because of personal and family problems, and two
residents moved to other floors because of a
roommate conflict that could not be resolved.
Of the remaining seventeen residents, eleven
will be returning to the university in the
spring semester. Five students are leaving the
system to study at a university closer to home,
and one is moving out of the dormitory into an
apartment. Five of the returning students will
move back to Barry Hall's second floor, while
six will be moving to other floors after having
been seriously frustrated by living on a non-
academic floor. This shows the variety of different stressful situations that can occur on a
dormitory floor.

Solutions

Although the dropout rate caused by stress
in the dormitories does not significantly affect
the university because most students are commuters, it is a problem which, if alleviated,
will help to solve the institution's overall
retention problem. At a time when UTEP is concerned with decreasing enrollments, maintaining
enrollments is important. The implementation of

generalized description of the problem related to the specific case

a wide range of educational and social program-
ming within the residence hall, strengthening
the programs of recruitment, admission, counseling services, financial aid, career planning and
placement, and health services will also
contribute to decreased stress and improved
retention.

It is imperative that those individuals who
have the closest contact with the resident
students--their resident assistants--be trained
in handling stress. Additionally, they must be
introduced thoroughly to the services available
on campus. Resident assistants can work closely
with, for instance, the New Students Relations
office to point out incoming freshmen who might
be prone to drop out. Resident assistants should
also be involved in the workings of the freshmen
orientation program and in other programs which
can help students. These programs and departments include Financial Aid, the Career Information Center, Counseling Services, the Health
Center, Placement Services, Student Association,
and Study Skills.

Resident assistants should pay particular
attention to their residents and watch for signs
which warn them if students are having stress-
related problems. If a resident assistant
suspects that a resident is having a special
problem, the resident can be referred to an
appropriate program or department for help.

With proper training resident advisors can
take the necessary steps to control the 50%
attrition rates among on-campus resident
students.

Student Stress   7

References

Bishop, J. B., & Snyder, G. S. (1976). Commuters and residents: Pressures, helps and psychological services. <u>Journal of College Student Personnel, 17,</u> 232-235.

Ecklund, B. K., & Henderson, L. B. (1981). <u>Longitudinal study of the high school class of 1972.</u> Washington, DC: National Institute of Education. (ERIC Document Reproduction Service No. ED 311 222).

Dusek, R., & Renteria, R. (1984, December 13). Plan slashes UTEP budget by 28%. <u>El Paso Times,</u> p. A1.

APA now recommends this format for all manuscripts submitted for publication. If your instructor prefers, you may type the first line of each entry flush with the left margin and indent each subsequent line three spaces.

SAMPLE
SOCIAL SCIENCE PAPER:
APA FORMAT

Running head: MATERNAL SMOKING

A Study of the Relationship of

Maternal Smoking During Pregnancy

to Low Birth Weight Among Infants Born in a

Massachusetts South Shore Hospital

June M. Fahrman

Social Science 352

Dr. Robert Spiegel

December 12, 1994

Maternal Smoking   2

Table of Contents

Page

A Study of the Relationship of

Maternal Smoking During Pregnancy

to Low Birth Weight Among Infants Born in a

Massachusetts South Shore Hospital

Introduction

Problem

Physicians agree that low-birth-weight
babies, indicated by those weighing less than
5.5 pounds, struggle to survive their infancy.
These infants are 40 times more likely to die
during the first 4 weeks of life than babies
born over this weight (Papalia & Olds, 1990:
138). According to the former Surgeon General,
C. Everett Koop, M.D., two-thirds of all babies
who die in their first year are low-birth-weight
infants.

The incidence of low birth weight is recognized as a major public health concern. When an
infant is born with low birth weight, it is more
vulnerable to numerous complications, many of
which lead to death. Those infants who do survive can be left with disabling conditions, both
physical and psychological. Evidence of underde-
veloped lungs, more susceptibility to infections, low blood sugar, jaundice, and bleeding
in the brain is found in low-birth-weight
infants (Papalia & Olds, 1990:138). In addition,
medical costs associated with treatment of these

and other complications are enormous. Health
insurance rates, for physicians and individuals,
have dramatically increased. Answers to questions regarding the reduction of risk factors
attribuatble to low birth weight can have significant value to physicians, insurance companies,
and the public.

Risk factors attributable to low birth
weight can be demographic, socioeconomic, and
associated with lifestyle. Lifestyle risk factors include poor nutrition, abuse of alcohol,
and smoking. Previous research studies have
concluded that there appears to be a relationship between these and other maternal risk
factors and the delivery of low-birth-weight
infants.

The present study will pursue the relationship of one particular lifestyle risk factor
during pregnancy, smoking, to the incidence of
low birth weight and attempt to confirm previous
studies that a direct positive correlation between the two exists. Women who smoke during
pregnancy are smoking for two. Through the placenta, the fetus receives toxic substances found
in tobacco smoke. By smoking, the woman also
reduces the oxygen supply to the fetus. When
blood vessels in the placenta are restricted due
to cigarette nicotine, nutrients to the fetus
are reduced. Decreased oxygen and nutrients to
the fetus reduces fetal growth. Pregnant women
who smoke, therefore, are more likely to give
birth to lower weight infants. If, on the other
hand, pregnant women do not smoke, one can
assume that they will be less likely to give

birth to lower weight infants.

Amenability to Study

    The relationship of maternal smoking during
pregnancy to low-birth-weight infants is limited
to bounds amenable to study. A review of the
literature provides the theoretical framework
for the present investigation. A combined
population of pregnant women at different age,
race, and economic levels as well as nurses and
physicians is available and accessible for the
study. Both probability/random and non-proba-
bility/non-random sampling procedures will be
used to enumerate the appropriate number of
respondents. The following major method will be
used to ascertain the data from the prospective
respondents: questionnaire. The obtained data
will be critically analyzed by descriptive and
inferential techniques.

    Finally, time and funding are of minimal
constraint in the present investigation, thus
providing further evidence that the problem
articulated above is limited to bounds amenable
to study.

Significance of Study

    The present study is significant from two
perspectives: pure and applied. From the pure
knowledge perspective, the findings of the
present study will contribute to the existing
literature in the following areas: health care,
psychology, business, and education, among
others. Furthermore, the results and conclusion
generated by this study would help to develop a
theoretical framework for further studies of the
relationship of maternal smoking during

pregnancy and the probability of low birth
weight among infants.

From the applied perspective, the findings
of the present study will help clarify the relationship of smoking during pregnancy to low
birth weight. Expected results of the study show
that mothers who smoke during pregnancy are more
likely to give birth to low weight infants.

With this finding, programs can be developed to minimize low birth weight through
smoking cessation. Physicians can educate pregnant women on the effects of their smoking and
the consequences of delivering low-birth-weight
babies, thus creating a motive for women to quit
smoking during pregnancy. Decreasing the number
of low-birth-weight infants can have a direct
impact on medical costs and health insurance
rates. Cessation programs and education would
help limit the number of smoking pregnant women,
thus reducing the number of low-birth-weight
infants and increasing the survival rate of such
infants.

Theoretical Framework

Review of Literature

A review of the literature suggests a positive correlation between smoking during pregnancy and low birth weight. In a recent study of
women in Puerto Rico, Becerra and Smith (1988)
attempted to examine the relationship of maternal smoking to low birth weight. They hypothe-
sized that the effect of maternal smoking on
birth weight is constant among different
socioeconomic and age groups in Puerto Rico and
that any effect of smoking on birth weight is

explained by constitutional factors. To test
their assumptions, Becerra and Smith used
secondary analysis obtained from the Puerto Rico
Fertility and Family Planning Assessment
(PRFFPA). The sampling scheme of the PRFFPA
included a two-stage stratified cluster sample
representative of the entire population of
Puerto Rico. Questionnaires were mailed to 4,500
households. A representative sample of 3,175
women were then interviewed. Respondents
selected for Becerra and Smith's study included
singleton births born in hospitals and whose
birth weights or birth dates were known. Becerra
and Smith focused on three questions that defined the prenatal smoking exposure of infants.
The respondents were asked if they currently
smoked. If they answered, "yes," they were asked
at what age they started smoking. If they
answered "no," they were asked if they had ever
been a cigarette smoker. Obtained data were
analyzed by simple descriptive techniques.
Births to mothers who started smoking regularly
at some time before delivery and who were still
smoking at the time of the interview were compared with births to mothers who did not smoke.
Becerra and Smith reported that births to
mothers who smoked during pregnancy aged 20 and
older delivering in public hospitals were 2.5
times more likely to weigh less than 2,500 grams
and on the average weighed 207 grams less than
births of a comparable group of non-smoking
mothers (1988:268). The research concluded that
there appears to be sufficient empirical evidence to support the assumption that maternal

smoking is associated with an increased risk of
low birth weight. Becerra and Smith's study
provides an essential theoretical framework for
the present investigation.

Similar conclusions were derived in a study
conducted by a team of researchers at the Division of Nutrition (Fichtner, Sullivan, Zyrkowski, & Trowbridge, 1990). The researchers were
interested in the relationship that smoking and
other risk factors have to low birth weight.
Nearly 248,000 records from the CDC's Pregnancy
Nutrition Surveillance System (PNSS) were analyzed by the Division of Nutrition. Records that
provided data on smoking; pregnancies that re-
sulted in live, singleton births; and infant
birth weight were used. Recorded smoking status
was ascertained by asking the question, "Are you
currently smoking cigarettes?" The data were
analyzed by simple descriptive methods. The
Division of Nutrition research team showed that
the low-birth-weight percentage for smokers was
9.9 compared to 5.7 for nonsmokers (Fichtner et
al., 1990:16). One weakness of the study, however, was that the prevalence of smoking is
higher among PNSS participants than it is in the
general population (Fichtner et al., 1990: 17).
Nevertheless, the research concluded that there
appears to be a correlation between the risk
factor, maternal smoking, and low birth weight.

Maternal smoking and its effect on birth weight was also studied by Sexton and Hebel (1984). Nine hundred thirty-five pregnant smokers from a large metropolitan area were randomly selected to participate in a clinical trial study. This study was conducted to test the hypothesis that a reduction in smoking during pregnancy would increase the birth weight of the infant. The women were randomly assigned to treatment and control groups. The intervention program was established and done primarily through individual contacts consisting of at least one personal visit and a monthly phone call. The percentage of women who reported not smoking cigarettes at the eighth-month contact was twice as high for the treatment group as for the control group, 43% and 20%, respectively (Sexton & Hebel, 1984:913). Hospital charts were used for the abstraction of birth-weight information. The data from the control group and treatment group were analyzed by one-way analysis of variance. Sexton and Hebel found for single, live births, the infants born to mothers in the treatment group had a mean birth weight of 3,278 grams, 92 grams heavier than the infants born to mothers in the control group and that the birth weight difference was statistically significant at P = < .05 (1984:913). Sexton and Hebel concluded that one of the major findings from their prospective, randomized, and controlled experiment suggests that cessation even during pregnancy improves the birth weight of the baby (1984:914).

In another prenatal smoking cessation study, Ershoff, Quinn, Mullen, and Lairson (1990) arrived at similar conclusions. A random sample of 323 smokers from five health centers in southern California were assigned to experimental and control groups. Experimental subjects were introduced to a serialized cessation program oriented to women and pregnancy. All medical care providers were blind to study group assignment (Ershoff et al., 1990:342). Hospital records were used to obtain birth weight. The obtained data were analyzed by using variance and covariance analysis. The team of researchers found that women assigned to the self-help cessation program were more likely to give birth to infants weighing, on average, 57 grams more than the infants born to women in the control group, and were 45% less likely to deliver a low-birth-weight infant (Ershoff et al., 1990: 340). The researchers concluded that there is strong evidence that supports a relationship between maternal smoking cessation and increasing birth weight.

In a final study reviewed, Shiono, Klebanoff, and Rhoads (1986) were interested in smoking and alcohol use during pregnancy and their effect on preterm births. (Preterm births have been associated with low birth weight in other studies.) The 30,598 women in the study were recruited from 13 Kaiser clinics serving

northern California. As part of their prenatal care
at Kaiser, the women had completed self-administered
questionnaires that included information on their use
of tobacco and alcohol. Kaiser's computerized records
were used to obtain pregnancy outcomes. Multiple
linear logistic regression was used to estimate the
adjusted odds ratios for preterm (<37 weeks) and very
preterm (<53 weeks) births. The researchers found
that preterm births were 20% more common in women
smoking at least one pack of cigarettes per day, and
the strongest effect was seen in very preterm births
in whom the excess was 60% (Shiono et al., 1386:82).
The study suggests that smoking during pregnancy
leads to preterm birth.

Hypothesis

In view of the above discussions and the review
of the literature, the present study will attempt to
provide empirical support to the thesis that mothers
who smoke during pregnancy are more likely to give
birth to low-weight infants. In other words, the
present study will provide evidence to support the
view that fetuses exposed to smoke will weigh less at
birth than fetuses who have not been exposed.

Operational Definitions

Concepts used in the hypothesis statement have
been operationally defined, in that they have been
reduced to the level where they can be measured
empirically. Formerly, mothers who smoked during
pregnancy were defined as pregnant women who inhaled

tobacco smoke. Operationally, this concept will
be measured by the following indices: Any
pregnant woman between the ages of 18 and 40
years, who was a prepregnant smoker and who
continued to smoke at the time of delivery a
minimum of one pack of cigarettes per week. The
dependent variable, low birth weight in infants,
is formally defined as a weight less than 5.5
pounds (2,500 grams) at birth (Papalia & Olds,
1990:137). Operationally, low birth weight in
infants will be measured in pounds and ounces
and converted to grams. Only singleton births
whose birth weights are between 1,000 and 2,000
grams will be included in the analysis.

Assumptions, Limitations, and Delimitations

     The major theoretical assumption guiding
the present investigation is that toxic substances in tobacco smoke pass through the placenta of a pregnant woman and reach her developing fetus. If the fetus is exposed to these
toxic substances, then there will be some adverse physiological change that will manifest in
the newborn. However, if on the other hand, the
fetus is not exposed to toxic substances, then
it will not have the adverse physiological
change in birth weight. More specifically, the
assumption is that the birth weight of newborns
will be lower if the mother smokes during
pregnancy.

     Time and funding will place several limi-
tations upon the present study, among which are
the following:

1.   Small sample size
2.   Not as comprehensive as a study could be

3. Restriction on the number of hospitals or
   clinics to be investigated

Other limitations reflect the homogeneous nature
of the sample that may not lend itself to generalization beyond the sample studied. The sample
will be selected from a white, middle-class
community in the South Shore area of Massachusetts. Respondents will be selected from only
one hospital, and thus will not be considered a
representative sample of the community. No
information regarding social economic status,
race, health education, time prenatal care
began, drinking during pregnancy, family background and history, and subjectivity to passive
smoke will be available, thus limiting the
ability of the present investigation to control
intervening or extraneous variables. In view of
the above limitations, the major delimitation of
the present study is its inability to generalize
the major finding and conclusions beyond the
sample population under scrutiny.

Methodology

Nature and Design of Study

The present study is descriptive in nature.
A descriptive study is the "defining and classi
fying of events and their relationships" (Bootzin & Acocella, 1988:116). More specific to the
present study, attempts will be made to describe
the relationship of maternal smoking to the
incidence of low birth weight.

The design of the present study is cross-
sectional. Papalia and Olds define a cross-
sectional study as "research that assesses different people of different ages at the same

time" (1990:40). Specifically, the present study will assess women who gave birth during the spring of 1991. The present investigation will be conducted in a community with a total population of 20,000 people and located in the southeastern part of Massachusetts.

Sampling Procedure

Selecting a sample is predicated upon a number of factors, among which include the availability, accessibility, receptivity, and the special qualifications of the prospective respondents. In view of the above constraints, the present study will use a random sampling procedure. More specifically, a simple random sample will be used to enumerate the appropriate pregnant women for the present investigation. In a simple random sample, a number is assigned to each population member; and using a table of random numbers, selections are made until the number of individuals needed for the study have been reached (Sanders & Pinhey, 1987:114-115).

For the present study, all women who had already given birth constitute the population of the study. The investigator will meet with four obstetricians of a South Shore hospital and discuss with them the proposed study. Upon the approval of the obstetricians, the investigator will receive a list of the names of women who gave birth during the spring of 1991. The next step would be to assign a number to each woman. Using a table of random numbers, 50 women from each list supplied by the four obstetricians will be selected. A total of 200 women will constitute the sample size.

Methods of Data Collection

Data needed to complete the present study will be obtained from the respondents by a survey method, specifically, a questionnaire. This particular method of data collection offers advantages over other methods:

1. Permits wide coverage for minimum expense
2. Permits more considered answers
3. Gives respondents a sense of privacy
4. Greater uniformity in the manner in which questions are posed
5. Provides responses that are easier to quantify than observations made in interviews

The questionnaire is designed in such a manner as to facilitate collection of data in the following areas:

1. Demographic characteristic: age of pregnant woman
2. Independent variable: smoking behavior of the woman before and during pregnancy
3. Dependent variable: birth weight of baby born to pregnant woman

A pretested questionnaire with a cover letter and a self-addressed stamped envelope will be mailed to each mother. The mother will be asked to complete the questionnaire and return it to the investigator by the deadline specified in the cover letter. A follow-up postcard will be mailed out to each mother thanking her for her cooperation in completing the study. Furthermore, a follow-up postcard promises to increase the number of returns.

<u>Method of Data Analysis</u>

Once all the questionnaires to be included in the analysis have been received, the first step in the analysis will be to tally all responses to each questionnaire item. Next, the questionnaire will be categorized into one of two groups:

1. Women who smoked during pregnancy
2. Women who did not smoke during pregnancy

Each respondent will be further classified into one of two groups:

1. Women giving birth to low-birth-weight infants (weighing less than 2,500 grams)
2. Women giving birth to non-low-birth-weight infants (weighing more than 2,500 grams)

Major relationships to be analyzed include the following:

1. Relationship of respondents to:
   a. smoking during pregnancy
   b. nonsmoking during pregnancy
2. Relationship of respondents to:
   a. giving birth to low-birth-weight infants
   b. giving birth to non-low-birth-weight infants
3. Relationship of smoking and nonsmoking during pregnancy to:
   a. low-birth-weight infants
   b. non-low-birth-weight infants

The relationship of the independent variable (smoking) and the dependent variable (low birth weight) will assume the following two-by-two format:

Maternal Smoking   17

Low Birth Weight

Smoking	Yes	No	Total
Yes	___	___	___
No	___	___	___
Total	___	___	___

Phi coefficient will be used to measure the association between smoking and low birth weight. Finally, chi-square test statistics will be used to test the null hypothesis of no difference between smoking and low birth weight.

Reliability and Validity

Reliability is concerned with consistency. If an instrument or a study consistently yields the same result, then the instrument or the study is said to possess reliability. Because the present study will not be repeated over a period of time, it would be somewhat problematic to establish its reliability. However, the pretested instrument of the present study would assure, at least to some extent, a measure of reliability of the present investigation.

The present study possesses face validity. By the professional judgment of the investigator, the present proposed study is said to possess validity. The present investigation is derived from an extensive review of the literature. The hypothesis and the operational definitions have sound theoretical underpinnings, thus assuring construct/external validity. Finally, the instrument has been pretested, contributing to the internal/content validity of the present study.

In summary, then, the present investigation is said to possess not only reliability but also validity.

Maternal Smoking   19

References

Becerra, J. E., & Smith, J. C. (1988).
Maternal smoking and low birthweight in the
reproductive history of women in Puerto Rico,
1982. American Journal of Public Health, 78,
268-272.

Bootzin, R. R., & Acocella, J. R. (1988).
Abnormal psychology: Current perspectives (5th
ed.). New York: Random House.

Ershoff, D. H., Quinn, V. P., Mullen, P.
D., & Lairson, D. R. (1990). Pregnancy and
medical cost outcomes of a self-help prenatal
smoking cessation program in an HMO. Public
Health Reports, 105(4), 340-347.

Fichtner, R. R., Sullivan, K. M.,
Zyrkowski, C. L., & Trowbridge, F. L. (1990).
Racial/ethnic differences in smoking, other risk
factors, and low birth weight among low-income
pregnant women, 1978-1988. Morbidity and
Mortality Weekly Report, 39(SS-3), 13-21.

Fox, S. H., Brown, C., Koontz, A. M., &
Kessel, S. S. (1987). Perceptions of risks of
smoking and heavy drinking during pregnancy:
1985 NHIS findings. Public Health Reports,
102(1), 73-79.

Monette, D. R., Sullivan, T. J., & DeJong,
C. R. (1990). Applied social research: Tool for
the human services (2nd ed.). Fort Worth: Holt,
Rinehart and Winston.

Papalia, D. E., & Olds, S. W. (1990).
A child's world: Infancy through adolescence
(5th ed.). New York: McGraw-Hill.

Sanders, J., & Pinehy, A. (1983). The conduct of social research. New York: Holt, Rinehart, and Winston.

Sexton, M., & Hebel, J. R. (1984). A clinical trial of change in maternal smoking and its effect on birth weight. Journal of the American Medical Association, 251(7), 911-915.

Shiono, P. H., Klebanoff, M. A., & Rhoads, G. G. (1986). Smoking and drinking during pregnancy. Journal of the American Medical Association, 255(1), 82-84.

U.S. Department of Health and Human Services (USDHHS). (1985). Smoking and pregnancy (DHHS Publication No. 85-89-P). Washington, DC: Government Printing Office.

APA now recommends this format for all mauscripts submitted for publication. If your instructor prefers, you may use hanging indents. See page 117.

Maternal Smoking   21

Appendix

Maternal Smoking   22

2 Thoreau Drive
South Easton, MA 02375
November 1, 1994

Dear Respondent's Name:

I am a student at Stonehill College and am
presently conducting a research study in partial
fulfillment of the requirements for my degree.
This study involves an analysis of smoking
during pregnancy.

Dr. Michael Baines, Chief of Obstetrics and
Gynecology, has granted me permission to conduct
this research among the patients of all four
obstetricians at BYU Hospital. A random sample
of fifty patients from each of the four obstetricians has been selected for this study. I am
happy to inform you that you were randomly
selected as a subject in this scientific
research investigation.

Please complete the attached questionnaire
and return it in the self-addressed stamped
envelope no later than December 28, 1994. Please
be assured that no respondent will be personally
identified in this study and that the information you provide me will be treated with the
utmost confidentiality.

If you have any questions, either about the
study or the attached questionnaire, please feel
free to call me at (508) 238-1135 and I will be
happy to answer them.

Thank you for your consideration. If you
desire a copy of the study results/findings,
please let me know and I will be most happy to
provide you with a copy.

Sincerely,

June M. Fahrman

Maternal Smoking   23

QUESTIONNAIRE

Please complete this questionnaire by checking
the appropriate responses or by providing the
needed information. Your candor is crucial to
this study.

1. Are you currently a smoker?
   ____ YES ____ NO

2. Did you smoke prior to your pregnancy?
   ____ YES ____ NO

   If you answered yes to question number 2, on
   the average, how much did you smoke prior to
   your pregnancy?

   ____ Less than one pack of cigarettes per day

   ____ One or more packs of cigarettes per day

3. Did you smoke during your pregnancy?

        YES   NO

   If you answered yes to question number 3, on
   the average, how much did you smoke during
   your pregnancy?

   ____ Less than one pack of cigarettes per day

   ____ One or more packs of cigarettes per day

Maternal Smoking   24

4. Did you deliver:
    ____ singleton birth (one baby)
    ____ multiple birth (two or more babies)

IF YOU HAD A SINGLETON BIRTH PLEASE ANSWER ALL
OF THESE QUESTIONS. IF YOU HAD A MULTIPLE BIRTH
PLEASE GO DIRECTLY TO QUESTION 8.

5. Sex of your baby: ____ Male   ____ Female

6. Length of infant at birth ____ Inches

7. Weight of infant at birth
    ____ Pounds ____ Ounces

8. How old were you at the time of delivery?
    ____ Years

If you have any additional information about
this study and/or if you wish to comment on this
study, please do so here:

WRITING IN
THE SCIENCES

Science writing consists largely of reviewing literature, reporting procedures and materials (so that they can be replicated), and discussing empirical results and their implications. Most methods of preparing protocols, reports, and literature reviews are common to other subjects. Although science writing may be persuasive, as in a paper arguing that computerized heat treatments are a superior method of treating metals, it is usually expository, concerned with accurately reporting observations and experimental data.

RESEARCH SOURCES

The methods of data collection in the sciences frequently entail observation and experimental research. Most results are tabulated and presented graphically. However, literature searches are often carried out in the library.

SPECIALIZED LIBRARY SOURCES

The following specific sources are just some of those available to the sciences.

General Science
Applied Science and Technology Index
CRC Handbook of Chemistry and Physics (and other titles in the CRC series of handbooks)
General Science Index
McGraw-Hill Encyclopedia of Science and Technology
Science Citation Index

Chemistry
Analytical Abstracts
Chemical Abstracts
Encyclopedia of Chemistry
Kirk-Othmer Encyclopedia of Chemical Technology

Engineering
Engineering Encyclopedia
Engineering Index
Environment Index
Government Reports Announcements (NTIS)
HRIS Abstracts (Highway Engineering)

Geology
Abstracts of North American Geology
Annotated Bibliography of Economic Geology
Bibliography and Index of Geology
Bibliography of North American Geology
GeoAbstracts (Geographical Abstracts)
Publications of the USCS
Selected Water Resources Abstracts

Life Sciences
Biological Abstracts
Biological and Agricultural Index
Encyclopedia of Bioethics
Encyclopedia of the Biological Sciences
Index Medicus

Mathematics
Index to Mathematical Papers
Mathematical Reviews
Universal Encyclopedia of Mathematics

Physics
Astronomy and Astrophysics Abstracts
Encyclopedia of Physics
Physics Abstracts
Solid State Abstracts Journal

The *Science Citation Index* lists authors and the publications in which their work has been cited. Scientists are particularly interested in the number of times and the variety of sources in which an author is cited and therefore use citation indexes frequently.

SPECIALIZED DATABASES FOR COMPUTER SEARCHES

As with other disciplines, many print indexes are also available on-line. Helpful databases for research in the sciences include *BIOSIS Previews, CASearch, SCISEARCH, Agvicola, CAB Abstracts, Compendex, NTIS, Inspec, MEDLINE, MATHSCI,* and *Life Sciences Collection.*

NON-LIBRARY SOURCES

As stated earlier, much of the research in the sciences is conducted in the laboratory or in the field. Non-library sources in the sciences vary greatly because of the many subjects that make up the sciences. In agronomy, for example, you might need to collect soil samples; in toxicology, you might want to test air or water quality. In marine biology, you might conduct research in a particular aquatic environment, while in chemistry you might collect blood samples.

ASSIGNMENTS IN THE SCIENCES

Many writing assignments in a science class are similar to those assigned in the other disciplines; for instance, they include annotated bibliographies (see "Writing in the Humanities") and proposals (see "Writing in the Social Sciences"). Two additional assignments common in (but not limited to) science disciplines are the abstract, the literature survey, and the laboratory report.

ABSTRACTS

Many scientific indexes provide abstracts of articles so that researchers may know whether an article is of specific use to them. Most scientific articles provide an abstract at the beginning of the article. Such an abstract serves as a road map or guide for readers. An *indicative abstract* merely indicates what the content of an article is. It helps readers decide whether they want to read the article in full or whether the contents of the article are of use to them. An *informative abstract* is detailed enough so that readers can obtain essential information without reading the article itself. Interpretation and criticism are usually not included in an abstract.

When writing an abstract, follow the organization of your paper. State the purpose, method of research, results, and conclusion in the order in which they occur in the paper, but include essential information only. An abstract should contain about 200-500 words. Avoid quoting from your paper or repeating the title. An abstract should also provide clear information for a wide audience; therefore, avoid overly technical vocabulary. Indicative abstracts are used in indexes, catalogs, and proposals. Informative abstracts are usually included in annotated bibliographies and summarized in literature survey sections. (An annotated bibliography is made up of short indicative abstracts that follow each complete citation in a bibliography.)

LITERATURE SURVEYS

Literature surveys are common to the social sciences—psychology, sociology, political science—and to the sciences. They are usually used in preparing project proposals or as precursors to arguments in a paper in which you might try to prove the uniqueness of your experimental method or your argument. Unlike an abstract, which simply gives the necessary information, a literature survey can be argumentative. A literature survey also does much comparison and contrast of the articles which the researcher has read. Here is a sample of a literature survey from a paper written for a biology course in parasitology.

Ultrastructural studies of micro- and macrogametes have included relatively few of the numerous Eimerian species. Major early studies include the following (hosts are listed in parentheses): micro- and macrogametes of E. perforans (rabbits), E. stiedae (rabbits), E. bovis (cattle), and E. auburnensis (cattle) (Hammond et al., 1967; Scholtyseck et al., 1966), macrogametogenesis in E. magna (rabbits) and E. intestinalis (rabbits) (Kheysin, 1965), macrogametogony of E. tenella (chickens) (McLaren, 1969), and the microgametocytes and macrogametes of E. neischulzi (rats) (Colley, 1967). More recent investigations have included macrogametogony of E. acervulina (chickens) (Pitillo and Ball, 1984).

There is little knowledge concerning the nutrient requirements of the Eimeria, but their parasitic nature is evidence for dependency on host nutrients. Warren (1969) utilized diet deficiency techniques to study the effect of various vitamins or growth factors on the course of E. tenella and E. acervulina infections in chickens. Deficiency in biotin led to a 90% reduction in oocyst production. Biotin, the essential cofactor in biosynthesis of fatty acids and fatty alcohols was found to be necessary for schizogony and gametogony in both parasites. Charney et al. (1971) found that a fatty acid deficient diet reduced the amount of lesions and mortality caused by E. tenella and E. mivati infections in chickens. When corn oil supplement was added the severity of the infection resumed, whereas hydrogenated coconut oil supplement did not counteract the deficiency. These results indicate that coccidia are unable to metabolize some of the essential unsaturated fatty acids. The localization of electron-dense ferritinbiotin complex in intravacuolar tubules would support the hypothesis that they are used for nutrient transport and that biotin is required.

Because new research begins where earlier research left off, research questions and hypotheses grow out of literature surveys. Therefore, these surveys are necessary for original research.

LABORATORY REPORTS

The laboratory report is perhaps the most common type of writing assigned to students taking courses in the sciences. It is divided into sections that generally conform to the specifications for a science paper outlined in this chapter. Not every section described in this format will be necessary for every experiment. Some experiments may even call for additional components, such as abstracts or references. In addition, a lab experiment will often include tables, charts, graphs, and illustrations. Much of the time, the exact format of a student lab report is defined by the lab manual being used in a specific course.

In general, a lab report is a process explanation. For this reason, explaining a process clearly and completely, with its steps in exact chronological order, and illustrating the purpose of each step are essential skills for students writing in the sciences. However, writing in a lab report is not limited to process explanation. The methods and materials section of a lab report requires that you clearly describe the equipment used in an experiment and explain its function (unless you can assume that it will be familiar to the intended reader). For instance, in a lab report you must not only describe how you set up a spirit level, but also explain the function of the specific tools you used. For example, you might parenthetically define the tools in this manner: "a hand level (a small device that allows the person looking through it to locate points at the same elevation levels as the device) and a Philadelphia rod (a graduated leveling rod with a movable marker)." In the end, the results you obtain from your experiment must be described precisely and discussed clearly.

CONVENTIONS OF STYLE AND FORMAT

The scientific researcher who publishes results of original research in a professional journal will often make use of the conventions of style and format required by the journal. Students reporting their own research will frequently be asked to follow conventions similar to those described below.

In writing your lab report or scientific paper, use the passive voice to emphasize tasks rather than the person performing them. Avoid using the second person—that is, avoid giving instructions and directions. It is acceptable to use the first person when writing about your own experiment. Direct quotations are not often used in scientific papers.

Think of the purpose of your writing as providing information for other scientists. This means that you should attempt to clarify your language so that scientists in different science disciplines can understand what you have written. Over-reliance on technical jargon can limit the clarity and communicability of your paper.

Typically, the science paper is divided into four main sections: introduction, materials and methods, results, and conclusion. These sections are often preceded by a title page and an abstract.

- The **introduction** should identify the question, formulate a testable hypothesis, state the purpose of the investigation, and mention briefly the general method of investigation used, perhaps explaining why this method was used over an alternative method. The introduction sometimes includes a literature survey.

- The **materials and methods section** lists equipment used and describes chronologically the steps of the experiment. It is a straightforward description of how you carried out your investigation. Often included in this discussion is a description of the equipment, the materials, and the method of collecting data.

- The **results section** presents a clear description of the data that you have collected. Quite often this section contains a graph of the data and a verbal summary of the results. Calculations, printouts, and other raw data are frequently presented in appendices. Note that this section should not present any conclusions.

• The **conclusion** presents an explanation of the results. It explains the importance of your results and may compare them with those discussed in the literature survey. In addition, you may explain any problems encountered in carrying out your experiment.

Tables and illustrations are an important part of most scientific papers. Some tables, illustrations, and graphs present results, while others may describe methods and materials. Tables should be placed as close to the discussion of them as possible. Even so, any type of illustration or diagram must be numbered and labeled clearly (Figure 1, for example) so that you can refer to it in your text.

DOCUMENTATION FORMATS

Documentation style varies from one scientific discipline to another; even within a given discipline, style may vary from one journal to another. For this reason, you should ask your instructor what documentation format is required. Most disciplines in the sciences use the formats prescribed by their professional societies. For instance, electrical engineers use the format of the Institute for Electronics and Electrical Engineers, chemists use the format of the American Chemical Society, physicists use the format of the American Institute of Physics, mathematicians use the format of the American Mathematical Society, and biologists use the format of the Council of Biology Editors.

THE CBE FORMAT*

CBE format is the documentation format recommended by the Council of Biology Editors and distributed by the American Institute of Biological Sciences. It is used by authors, editors, and publishers in biology, botany, zoology, physiology, anatomy, and genetics. It offers two options for documentation: author-date

---

*CBE documentation format follows the guidelines set in the *CBE Style Manual*, 5th ed. Bethesda, Md., Council of Biology Editors, 1983.

and number-reference. Since the author-date format has already been illustrated for APA style, the number-reference format will be illustrated here.* This format is similar to the formats used in the applied and medical sciences. Numbers inserted parenthetically in the text correspond to a reference list at the end of the paper. Works are arranged either alphabetically or in the order in which they are mentioned in the text and then numbered consecutively. When a list of references is typed, all lines begin at the left margin.

• **In the paper**

```
One study (1) has demonstrated the effect of low
dissolved oxygen. Cell walls of. . . .
```

• **In the reference list**

```
Name    Initials   Title not underlined (only first word capitalized)
  ↓        ↓              ↓
1. White, R. P.   An introduction to biochemistry.
   Philadelphia: W. B. Saunders; 1974.
        ↓              ↓             ↓
      City        Publisher        Date
```

Sample Citations: Books
For book entries, list the author(s), the title (with only the first word capitalized), the city of publication (followed by a colon), the name of the publisher (followed by a semicolon), and the year (followed by a period). Do not underline book titles.

A book with one author

```
1. Rathmil, P. D.  The synthesis of milk and
   related products.  Madison, WI: Hugo Summer;
   1985.
```

A book with more than one author

```
2. Krause, K. F.; Paterson, M. K., Jr.  Tissue
   culture: methods and application.  New York:
   Academic Press; 1973.
```

*Single spacing has been used in the references to save space.

An edited book

> 3. Marzacco, M. P., editor. A survey of
> biochemistry. New York: R. R. Bowker; 1985.

A specific edition of a book

> 4. Baldwin, L. D.; Rigby, C. V. A study of
> animal virology. 2nd ed. New York: John
> Wiley; 1984:121-133.

Sample Citations: Articles
For journal articles, list the author(s), the title of the article (with only the first word capitalized), the title of the journal (with all major words capitalized, not underlined), the volume number (followed by a colon), the inclusive page numbers of the article, and the year (followed by a period).

An article in a scholarly journal with continuous pagination in each issue

> 1. Bensley, L. Profiling women physicians. Medica
> 1:140-145; 1985.

An article in a scholarly journal that has separate pagination in each issue

> 2. Wilen, W. W. The biological clock of insects.
> Sci. Amer. 234(2):114-121; 1976.

An article with a subtitle

> 3. Schindler, A.; Donner, K. B. On DNA: the
> evolution of an amino acid sequence. J. Mol.
> Evol. 8:94-101; 1980.

An article with no listed author

> 4. Anonymous. Developments in microbiology.
> Int. J. Microbiol. 6:234-248; 1987.

An article with discontinuous pagination

    5. Williams, S.; Heller, G. A. Special dietary
       foods and their importance for diabetics. Food
       Prod. Dev. 44:54-62, 68-73; 1984.

OTHER SCIENCE FORMATS

In preparing your paper, remember that although the *Council of Biology Editors' Style Manual* governs the overall presentation of papers in biology, *The Journal of Immunology* might have a different format from the *The Journal of Parasitology*. (The *CBE Style Manual* lists the different journals that use its own style formats.) Your teacher may ask you to prepare your paper according to the style sheet of the journal to which you wish to submit your work. Although publication may seem a remote possibility to you, the fact that various groups use different formats underscores the fact that the readers in those groups use that format as a language for understanding one another. Browsing in the disciplinary area will make you familiar with the differences between each discipline.

Each professional society also prescribes the formats of charts and the way they are to be referred to in the text. Therefore, it is difficult to use one format for all the sciences. Also important to learn are the various abbreviations with which journals are referred to in the reference sections of science papers. For example: The American Journal of Physiology is abbreviated Amer. J. Physiol. and The Journal of Physiological Chemistry is abbreviated J. of Physiol. Chemistry. Note that in the CBE reference list, the abbreviated forms of journal titles are not underlined. Since elaborate rules exist for creating abbreviations—for instance, you should always add a consonant to your abbreviation (biol., not bio. for biology)—consult the appropriate style sheet if you have questions.

Journals in the sciences use a variation of either the number-reference system or the author-date system. However, it is imperative that the citations be consistent with the practice of the journal, for this means that they are consistent with the practice of researchers in the field.

1. The *author-date system* requires you to note the authors' last names and date of publication of the works you cite in your paper: "Smith and Jones (1980) conducted the following research. . . ." These citations are keyed to an alphabetical list of references at the end of the paper. (See the sample paper on page 191 for an example of the author-date format.)

2. The *number-reference system* requires you to list all the works used (in alphabetical order or in order of use) and assign each a number. Then, whenever you cite the author, you provide the number of that specific reference. (See sample paper on page 175.)

Here is a list of some common documentation styles used in various science disciplines.

American Institute of Physics. *Style Manual.* American Institute of Physics, 1990.

American Mathematical Society. *Manual for Authors of Mathematical Papers,* 6th ed. Providence, R.I.: The Society, 1984.

American Medical Association-Scientific Publications Division. *Stylebook: Editorial Manual.* Littleton, Mass.: Publishing Sciences Group, 1976.

Conference of Biology Editors. *Style Manual for Biological Journals,* 2nd ed. Washington, D.C.: American Institute of Biological Sciences, 1964.

Council of Biological Editors. *Style Manual: A Guide for Authors, Editors and Publishers in the Biological Sciences,* 5th ed. Arlington, Va.: American Institute of Biology Editors, 1983.

Dodd, Janet S., ed. *The ACS Style Manual.* Washington, D.C.: American Chemical Society, 1986.

SAMPLE PAPERS IN THE SCIENCES

The first student paper, "Shell Selection by Intertidal Hermit Crabs in the Gulf of California," follows the format of a science research report and illustrates the CBE number-reference format. The second student paper, "The Study of Fossil Flowers," illustrates the author-date format. The third student paper is a chemistry lab report which follows the format used to report research in professional chemistry journals. Since it reports primary research only, it does not use documentation.

SAMPLE SCIENCE PAPER: CBE FORMAT

Shell Selection by Intertidal Hermit Crabs
in the Gulf of California

Russell R. Broaddus, Marcia L. Hansel,
and Jennifer Richer

Correspondence: Jennifer Richer
                 Department of Biological Sciences
                 The University of Texas at El Paso
                 El Paso, Texas 79968

Shell Selection

1

Abstract

This study was designed to determine if shell
selection by hermit crabs is due to actual
preference for a specific shell species or based
on shell availability only. The hermit crabs and
snail shells were collected in two ecologically
different intertidal zones at Puerto Peñasco,
Sonora, Mexico. Five species of hermit crabs
were found principally in seven different
species of snail shells. <u>Clibanarius panamensis</u>
and <u>Pylopagurus roseus</u> demonstrated true shell
selection, while <u>Pagurus lepidus</u> and <u>Clibanarius
diqueti</u> selected specific shells as a second
choice of habitat. The shell's physical
characteristics, such as aperture size and
weight, and environmental conditions, such as
intertidal currents, predators, and habitat
complexity, affect a hermit crab's choice of a
specific shell.

*states
the
specific
purpose,
procedure,
and con-
clusions
of the
study*

*conclusion
drawn
from the
study*

Index descriptors: intertidal hermit crabs;
shell selection; Gulf of California, <u>Clibanarius
diqueti</u>, <u>Paguristes anahuacus</u>, <u>Pagurus lepidus</u>,
<u>Pylopagurus roseus</u>, <u>Cerithium maculosum</u>,
<u>Cerithium stercusmuscarum</u>, <u>Morula</u> sp.,
<u>Tegula</u> sp., <u>Turbo</u> sp.

*identifies
species
used and
scientific
classifi-
cation*

Shell Selection

2

Hermit crabs, the anomurans, belong to the order Decapoda and the class Crustacea. Hermit crabs differ from true crabs, the brachyurans, in that they possess an unusually soft, curved abdomen (Fig. 1). Lacking well developed pleopods, the locomotor value of this type of abdomen is greatly reduced. The hermit crab's solution to the problem of protecting this vulnerable abdomen is to inhabit an empty gastropod shell (Fig. 2). Apparently abandoned shells are used, as no aggression against a living snail has been documented (1, p. 432). However, many cases of hermit crabs battling over a potential home or a dominant crab evicting a weaker one from a more desirable shell have been observed in nature as well as in the laboratory (5, 6, 12, 13).

The non-land living hermit crabs are found in the intertidal zone. Since they are scavengers feeding on detritus, an important factor in their environment is the continual replenishment of food brought in by the sea. The intertidal environment is a dramatic habitat and organisms living in it must be able to tolerate environmental extremes and protect themselves from predation, desiccation, abrasion by wave action, and temperature variation. Therefore, the hermit crab uses the gastropod shell to serve as a "microhabitat" in which it can comfortably reside in the intertidal zone (10). Hermit crabs have been reported to carefully choose gastropod shells, exhibiting a complex behavioral routine before accepting a shell (9).

classification helps define the specific subject being studied

description and characteristics of the hermit crab

the numbers in parentheses refer to works listed in the Literature Cited

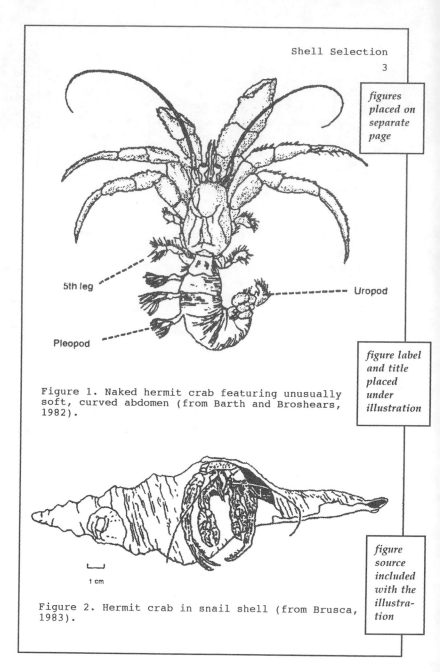

figures placed on separate page

5th leg

Pleopod

Uropod

Figure 1. Naked hermit crab featuring unusually soft, curved abdomen (from Barth and Broshears, 1982).

figure label and title placed under illustration

1 cm

Figure 2. Hermit crab in snail shell (from Brusca, 1983).

figure source included with the illustration

Researchers have discovered that hermit crabs are found more frequently in some species of shell than in others (2, 4, 8, 11, 12, 13). Therefore, it is apparent that hermit crab distribution in gastropod shells is not random. The important question lies in whether or not actual preference is occurring whereby specific species of hermit crabs select particular species of gastropod shells, or if they are simply choosing the most abundant species of shell available. The present study was designed to examine shell selection by hermit crabs in two different intertidal environments on the coast of the Gulf of California in Puerto Peñasco, Sonora, Mexico, and to determine if the distribution of the various species of hermit crabs in the indigenous species of gastropod shells was indicative of actual shell preferences or if shell selection was based on shell availability alone.

refers to several sources at once, indicating that several researchers have made similar observations

statement of purpose

Materials and Methods

Hermit crabs were collected at two ecologically different sites in Puerto Peñasco, Sonora, Mexico. One site was near the Centro de Estudios de Desiertos y Oceanos (CEDO) and the other, approximately 2 miles away, was near the Garcia House. The collection site near CEDO consisted of Coquina limestone reef flats with depressions and very few boulders. These reef flats were interspersed with large sand bars. The continental shelf gradually declined, resulting in shallow tidal pools with an unstable environment due to fluctuating water

details and description of the site of the study

temperature and increased tide disturbance. The Garcia House site, on the other hand, consisted of a large sand bar covered with boulders, followed by a large Coquina limestone reef to the seaward. Furthermore, the continental shelf sharply declined, forming deeper tide pools and providing a more stable environment with relatively constant water temperatures and less tidal disturbance.

Morning collections were made at CEDO during low tide while collections at the Garcia House were made during the evening low tide. A transect line was stretched from the shore to the low tide point. The radius of collection ranged from 1-6 m along the transect, depending on how far out the tide was and the abundance of shells in the area. The transect line was moved for each collection so as not to deplete the hermit crab population.

description of procedur used to collect specimens

Both the inhabited and the empty snail shells were collected in buckets of sea water and transported to the CEDO lab for crab and snail identification. The crabs were identified in the shell whenever possible, but if a crab could not be seen, the shell was held directly up to a dissecting microscope light, allowing one to see through the shell to determine if a crab inhabited it. If a crab was present inside the shell, the shell was placed on a hot plate, which stimulated the crab to leave its shell. Identification of the hermit crabs and snail shells was according to Brusca (3, p. 280). As

page number included with reference number

soon as identification was completed, the hermits and the shells were returned to their
original site in the sea.

Results

Five species of hermit crabs were found
predominantly in seven different species of
snail shells collected from CEDO and the Garcia
House. Table I shows that <u>Clibanarius digueti</u>
and <u>Paguristes anahuacus</u> were the most populous
hermit crabs at CEDO and the Garcia House,
respectively. <u>Cerithium stercusmuscarum</u> snail
shells were by far the most abundant at CEDO,
whereas <u>Turbo</u> and <u>Morula</u> shells were the most
abundant at the Garcia House (Table II). From
these tables, it can be seen that <u>Cerithium
masculosum</u> and <u>Morula</u> shells were rarely
inhabited at CEDO, even though both shells were
common at this location.

references to tables provides the scientists the chance to examine the evidence

At CEDO, <u>Pagarus lepidus</u>, <u>P. anahuacus</u> and
<u>Clibanarius panamensis</u> all preferred <u>C.
stercusmuscarum</u> shells. However, at the Garcia
House, <u>P. lepidus</u> mainly inhabited <u>Morula</u>,
<u>Tegula</u> and <u>Turbo</u> shells. <u>Pylopagurus roseus</u>, a
rare inhabitant at CEDO and the Garcia House,
chose <u>Tegula</u> and <u>Turbo</u> shells at both locations.

lists the results briefly; the discussion section analyzes the results

Shell Selection

7

TABLE I. Number of hermit crabs collected at Centro de Estudios de Desiertos y Oceanos and the Garcia House in Puerto Peñasco, Sonora, Mexico, on October 12-16, 1986.

	LOCATION	
HERMIT CRAB HOUSE	CEDO	GARCIA
Clibanarius diqueti	461	54
Clibanarius panamensis	45	23
Dardanus sinistripes	0	9
Paquristes anahuacus	123	139
Paqurus lepidus	243	78
Pylopaqurus roseus	11	7

tables placed on separate page, following the reference on page 6

TABLE II. Number of the most abundant snail shells (inhabited and empty) collected at Centro de Estudios de Desiertos y Oceanos and the Garcia House in Puerto Peñasco, Sonora, Mexico, on October 12-16, 1986.

	LOCATION	
SNAIL SHELL HOUSE	CEDO	GARCIA
Cerithium maculosum	140	22
Cerithium stercusmuscarum	1112	18
Columbella sp.	15	88
Morula sp.	189	340
Olivella sp.	49	14
Tequla sp.	48	168
Turbo sp.	44	355
Turitella sp.	24	2

table's label and title placed above the illustration

Shell Selection

8

Discussion

Upon first inspection, the results seem to
indicate that shell selection by hermit crabs is
non-specific--the crabs simply inhabit the most
abundant snail shell in their area. However, two
of the five species of hermit crabs collected
did exhibit specific shell selection. Pylopa-
gurus roseus chose principally Tegula and Turbo
shells at both CEDO and the Garcia House, even
though neither shell was common at CEDO. Tegula
and Turbo shells both have large percula, therefore, it may be that P. roseus preferred these
shells because it has a large, flat, major chela
that can act as an operculum to seal the large
opening against intruders. Clibanarius pana-
mensis also exhibited some shell selection.

There are several possible reasons why one
species of shell might be preferred over others.
At CEDO, Morula and C. maculosum shells were
rarely inhabited, even though they were the
second and third most populous shells, respectively. It may be that Morula shells were not
chosen because they are too small to protect the
crab or they are not heavy enough to stabilize
the crab during tidal currents.

Other investigators have also concluded
that the physical characteristics of a shell
influence shell selection by hermit crabs. The
type of shell inhabited by a crab is important
because the shell size and shape can influence
the crab's growth (2). Reese (8) found that
hermit crabs can discriminate between shells of

*literature
survey
compares
findings
with
existent
literature*

different snail species and between shells of different weights but of the same species. A heavy shell may be more preferable because it would prevent the crab from being washed away or crushed by the surf (10). Blackstone observed that small crabs have a strong preference for high-spired shells (2). The shell also protects the hermit from predation by fish, birds, brachyura crabs, and octopi (10), so a large shell operculum would endanger the hermit. Vance (13) observed that brachyurans mostly attacked hermits living in smaller shells that leave more of the crab exposed and also that hermits living in larger shells enjoyed greater protection.

A hermit crab may inhabit the most abundant snail shell in a region because it actually prefers that shell over other shells. If that particular shell is abundant in an area, then its corresponding crab may also live in that area. For instance, C. digueti was the most populous crab at CEDO, but only the third most populous at the Garcia House (Table III). The shell C. digueti inhabited at CEDO was the most abundant but it was only the sixth most abundant at the Garcia House. Thus, C. digueti was not common there. Pagurus lepidus was the second most populous crab at both locations, since one of its two favorite shells was abundant at both places (Table III). Paguristes anahuacus was the most numerous hermit at the Garcia House, but it was only the third most populous at CEDO; its three preferred shells at the Garcia House were not common at CEDO.

reference to the table in the paper

Shell Selection

10

table within paper following discussion and reference on page 9

TABLE III. Occurrence of hermit crabs in snail shells collected at Centro de Estudios de Desiertos y Oceanos in Puerto Peñasco, Sonora, Mexico, on October 12-16, 1986.

SNAILS	C. digueti	C. pana- mensis	P. ana- huacus	P. lepidus	P. roseus
C. macu- losum	73	1	8	1	1
C. stercus- muscarum	357	30	98	165	0
Columbella sp.	0	0	0	2	0
Morula sp.	12	11	10	51	0
Olivella sp.	1	2	2	18	2
Tegula sp.	9	0	1	1	4
Turbo sp.	8	0	1	1	4
Turitella sp.	0	0	2	2	0
Acanthina angelica	0	1	1	0	0
Agaronia testacea	0	0	0	1	0
Eupleura muricifornes	0	0	0	1	0
Solenosteina capitanea	1	0	0	0	0
Total Crabs	461	45	123	243	11

CRABS

conclusio

It is, therefore, the conclusion of the authors that shell selection by hermit crabs is a specific process. Although certain features (such as operculum size or weight) of the snail shell may explain why a certain shell is not selected, it is difficult to determine why a specific shell is selected.

Since our results indicate that environment affects snail shell distribution, which in turn affects hermit crab population (11), we advise that future work on hermit crab shell selection should include ecologically different collection sites. Environmental features such as current, predators, and habitat complexity affect the snail shell population and, thus, the hermit crab population (12). A physically diverse habitat increases the number of hermits in an area, because snails prefer to live in complex habitats. Therefore, shell selection studies conducted in the laboratory (8, 4) may not produce accurate results, because environmental factors influence hermit crabs' choice of a specific shell in a particular region.

Acknowledgments

The authors wish to express their gratitude to Maggie Waldmann and Joyous Nicholopoulos for the use of their snail shell collections, which were invaluable in identification.

Shell Selection
12

References

1. Barth, R. H.; Broshears, R. E. The inverte-
   brate world. Philadelphia: Saunders College
   Publishing; 1982.
2. Blackstone, N. W. The effects of shell size
   and shape on growth and form in the hermit
   crab _Pagurus longicarpus_. Biol. Bull. 168:
   75-90; 1985.
3. Brusca, R. C. Common intertidal inverte-
   brates of the Gulf of California. Tucson,
   AZ: University of Arizona Press; 1980.
4. Grant, W. C., Jr. Notes on the ecology and
   behavior of the hermit crab, _Pagurus aca-
   dianus_. Ecol. 44:767-771; 1963.
5. Hazlett, B. A. Interspecific shell fighting
   between _Pagurus bernhardus_ and _Porgurus
   cuanensis_ (Decapoda, Paguridea). Inv. Zool.
   29:215-220; 1967.
6. Hazlett, B. A. Effects of crowding on the
   agnostic behavior of the hermit crab,
   Pagurus bernhardus. Ecol. 49:573-575; 1968.
7. Mesce, K. A. Calcium-bearing objects elicit
   shell selection behavior in a hermit crab.
   Science 215:993-995; 1982.

capital letter in first word of title

title of journal abbreviated

Shell Selection

13

8. Reese, E. S. Shell selection behavior of hermit crabs. Anim. Behav. 10:337-360; 1962.

title of journal not underlined

9. Reese, E. S. The behavioral mechanisms underlying shell selection by hermit crabs. Anim. Behav. 21:78-126 1963.

10. Reese, E. S. Behavioral adaptations of intertidal hermit crabs. Amer. Zool. 9: 343-355; 1969.

11. Spight, T. M. Availability and use of shells by intertidal hermit crabs. Biol. Bull. 162: 120-133; 1977.

12. Vance, R. R. Competition and mechanism of coexistence in three sympatric species of intertidal hermit crabs. Ecol. 53: 1062-1074; 1972a.

two works by the same author in the same year

13. Vance, R. R. The role of shell adequacy in behavioral interactions involving hermit crabs. Ecol. 53:1075-1083; 1972b.

SAMPLE SCIENCE PAPER: AUTHOR–DATE FORMAT

The Study of Fossil Flowers

by

Karen McCracken

Biology 241

Plant Systematics

Dr. Steven Seavey

Spring 1984

Abstract

The discovery of the earliest fossil angiosperm
will be able to tell paleobotanists much about
the evolution of flowers. The earliest accepted
traces of angiosperms tell us that they existed
about 120 million years ago. As paleobotanists
pursue their search for fossil flowers, they
encounter technical difficulties as well as
difficulties with the current Linnean system of
classification.

For hundreds of years, scientists have been fascinated with the seemingly sudden rise and diversification of angiosperms, or flowering plants, during the late Mesozoic era. So far the earliest accepted traces of flowering plants have been found about 120 million years ago in the Lower Cretaceous period of the geologic time scale (see Appendix). Before this time, it was the gymnosperms--plants that have no true flowers, such as pines--that were abundant, but in increasing numbers and complexity fossil angiosperms can be found in later Cretaceous rocks. Most of the early angiosperm record consists of pollen, seeds, fruits, and leaf parts of the angiosperm. Fossil flowers are not as common because the delicate structures were less likely to be preserved. Still, paleobotanists continue to search for the most ancient flower. This paper will look at the importance of studying fossil flowers, what has been found, and what difficulties have been encountered while studying fossil flowers.

Fossil flowers can reveal extremely important information about the time, place, and biological origin of angiosperms. Also, fossil flowers are of particular interest to paleobotanists since modern-day classification of angiosperms is based primarily on floral morphology; seeds, pollen, and leaf morphology are of only secondary importance. With what we learn from each newly discovered fossil flower we can test the many hypotheses about primitive

flowers that are made based on living angiosperms.

Paleobotanists ultimately want to reveal
the origin of the angiosperm, but there are
several questions surrounding this general
search for the origin of flowering plants. First
of all, paleobotanists wish to know where and
when angiosperms arose (Hughes 1976b). This can
be answered by where flowers are found in geologic strata and what other types of fossils are
found with them. Also of significance to scientists is finding the family to which the primitive flower belongs, or, in other words, which
family of modern-day angiosperms is the most
primitive; recent literature indicates that this
is the most immediate question to be resolved
(Basinger and Dilcher 1984; Dilcher et al. 1976;
Friis and Skarby 1982; Hughes 1976b; Tiffney
1977). In 1915, Charles Bessey suggested that
the most ancient flower resembled flowers like
the magnolias that are large, bisexual, and
insect pollinated, but others thought that the
first angiosperms were small, unisexual, and
wind pollinated (Dilcher and Crane 1984). Although most botanists side with Bessey, this
debate has yet to be resolved by what can be
found in fossil flowers (Dilcher and Crane
1984). One question that is raised by this argument is whether the most primitive flowers were
pollinated by insects or wind. Since gymnosperms
are primarily pollinated by wind and 85% of
angiosperms are pollinated by insects, the
answer could reveal information about the

genetic lines along which angiosperms originated. Whether the first angiosperms were wind
or insect pollinated can be answered by the
morphology of fossil flowers. Another question
pertaining to the evolution of angiosperms that
could be resolved by further evidence is whether
the flowering plants arose monophyletically or
otherwise (Beck 1976). Finally, botanists are
confronted with the difficulty of finding
fossils to confirm their own speculations about
the origin of angiosperms (Dilcher et al. 1976).
To answer these many questions paleobotanists
continue their search for the most primitive
fossil flower.

In view of the fact that few fossil flowers
have been found as yet, the ultimate goal to
find enough evidence to explain the evolution of
angiosperms seems unattainable. The most major
fossil finds have been made in the past decade.
Three various flower types are represented by
mid-Cretaceous fossil flowers. The fossils have
been dated as far back as Cenomanian age. Pollen
and leaf fossils are the only evidence that
angiosperms existed before this time. This evidence will be briefly discussed later. The
diversity of the early fossil flowers appearing
in the same age indicates that divergence
occurred early in the history of angiosperms.

The most complete fossil flower was found
in Nebraska in the locality of Rose Creek
(Basinger and Dilcher 1984; Dilcher and Crane
1984). This flower is symmetrical with five
sepals and five petals. The sepals are joined at

the base and form a stiff shallow cup. The showy
petals are about half an inch long and spread
out, alternating with the sepals. There are also
five stamens and five carpels. The stamens have
stout filaments and massive anthers which spread
out, lying against the petals. The pollen grains
found with these fossil flowers are extremely
small (8 to 12 microns in diameter) with three
sculpturing furrows. Between the base of the
stamens and carpels is a ring of swollen tissue
that is believed to have produced nectar, indicating insect pollination. These fossil flowers
are most closely related to three living orders
of angiosperms--Saxifragales (Rosidae), Rosales
(Rosidae), and Rhamnales (Rosidae). Although
similar to these orders, the fossil flower could
not be placed in any one of these orders since
none have the same floral features.

Another fossil flower, most like flowers of
the order Magnoliales, has been found in Kansas
and is of similar age to the previously described fossil flower (Dilcher and Crane 1984).
This is a large, solitary flower borne at the
end of a leafy shoot. The diameter of the flower
is five to six inches with three outer sepals
and six to nine petals. The fossil shows scars
where the stamens were once attached. There are
believed to be 150 carpels which each contain
about 100 ovules, but only 20 to 40 developed
into seeds. Botanists believe that this flower
was insect pollinated because it was large and
radially symmetrical. The leaf structure

suggests that this fossil flower belongs to an
extinct species because the leaf resembles no
leaf of any living angiosperm.

The third fossil flower is most widespread
(Dilcher and Crane 1984). Many small, apparently
unisexual flowers make up a spheroidal head
about one-quarter of an inch in diameter. About
thirty-six heads are arranged in regular inter-
vals on a long axis. If there are any sepals or
petals, they are too small to be seen in the
fossil. The flowers have anywhere from four to
seven carpels. Most fossils show no sign of
stamens; however, similar flowers found in the
USSR appear to have produced pollen. The morphology suggests wind pollination. This fossil
flower is most similar to the genus <u>Platanus</u> or
the sycamores.

Fossils of secondary structures such as
stems and leaves are more abundant than the
flower parts since they are more easily preserved in the geologic strata. The earliest
evidence indicating that angiosperms existed
before Cenomanian time are miospore fossils,
which are found in Berriasian and Valanginian
ages (Hughes 1967b). These are fossils of spores
or pollen of unknown function. These miospore
fossils provide no conclusive evidence of the
existence of angiosperms at the time. A small
fruit, <u>Onoana california</u>, found in marine strata
of Barremian age, is one of the most important
discoveries to paleobotanists (Hughes 1976b).
The genus was newly formed and placed in the

family Icacinaceae. This family is not regarded
as primitive but fossils of this family have
been found in Eocene deposits. A smaller
species, O. nicanica, has also been found in
Aptian age strata in the USSR (Hughes 1976b).
Fossil leaves and woody structures have been
found with increasing abundance in later geo-
logical periods.

Paleobotanists confront several difficulties in their search for the earliest angiosperms. One of the major problems in solving the
angiosperm mystery through fossil flowers is the
scarcity of the fossils themselves. The more
abundant, widely disseminated and robust the
plant part, the more likely it is to be preserved (Dilcher and Crane 1984). Because the
cutin-covered surfaces of the secondary structures (stems, leaves, seeds, and the walls of
the spores and pollen grain) are designed to
keep water out, these parts are more easily
preserved than the reproductive parts of the
flower. Consequently the majority of the fossil
information is found in the secondary structures, which reveal little information (Hughes
1976b). Fossils of early Cretaceous show only
single organs or fragments and the numbers
increase steadily until whole plants can be
found in Turonian age (Hughes 1976a). Aside from
the difficulty in preservation, another explanation for the lack of fossil flowers may be the
location of origin of the first angiosperm. If
flowers first originated in upland areas where

there are no soil deposits, as opposed to aggra-
dational areas such as deltas, then the preservation of flowers would be very rare.

Some general problems of data handling must
be resolved before many of the questions about
angiosperm origin can be answered. Most of the
work with fossil flowers goes directly into
comparative morphology of living angiosperms
(Basinger and Dilcher 1984; Cronquist 1968;
Dilcher et al. 1976; Hughes 1976b). Although
this is an important aspect in the study of
fossil flowers, the tendency is often to over-
look evolutionary elements. The scientific
belief that the "present is the key to the past"
allows botanists to assume many things about
primitive flowers and their evolution. This
belief can lead to many obstacles when parallels
between extinct and living species of angiosperms are drawn too closely (Hughes 1976a). The
current system for handling fossil data is the
Linnean system, which is the classification
system used for modern-day flowering plants.
Norman Hughes (1976b) suggests that this system
is inadequate for paleontological material. He
believes that a system needs to be designed
where fossils can be conveniently analyzed and
compared. Otherwise, as the system is now,
retrieval is too difficult. Hughes' proposed
paleontological system would provide time-
correlation, geographic limits of the rock from
which the specimen is taken, and the nomencla-
ture for the specimen. This system could be

helpful in comparison of fossils and would allow
for easy data retrieval. Placing fossil flowers
in the Linnean system forces botanists to find
the family to which the fossil belongs. Often a
fossil cannot be affiliated to one family
because it is a representative of an extinct
family. Another problem that hinders the study
of fossil flowers is categorizing the actual
structure of the flower as primitive or
advanced. First of all, there may be differing
views on what is primitive (Beck 1976). As
mentioned earlier, most botanists believe a
magnolia-type flower is most primitive but some
also believe that a much smaller, unisexual
flower is more primitive. For the most part,
however, the analysis of a fossil flower as
primitive or advanced has been helpful in
separating fossil flowers from extant flowers
(Hughes 1976b).

The fossil flowers have been useful in
confirming most morphologists' belief of what is
a primitive angiosperm (Dilcher et al. 1976),
but still there are some questions. Both insect
and wind pollination existed in the earliest
fossil flowers, as seen earlier in the description of the fossils. Further evidence of earlier
ages needs to be found to confirm which form of
pollination is most primitive. Fossils of later
years can reveal much about the coevolution of
insects and flowers which brings up another
interesting area of study in fossil flowers
(Crepet 1984). Paleobotanists have been able to

determine that angiosperms first occurred at low
latitudes in tropical areas. But the most
important question about the time of origin
still remains unanswered, although evolution
must have taken place before mid-Cretaceous as
suggested by the diversity in the fossils found
in Cenomanian age and other fossil finds before
that age (Crepet 1984; Cronquist 1968; Dilcher
et al. 1976; Hughes 1976a). Finally, as far as
the biological origin of angiosperms is concerned, there is still much speculation. Perhaps
angiosperms have arisen from an undiscovered
extinct seed plant, or from gymnosperms, but
little evidence supports these hypotheses.
Further study of the morphology of fossil
flowers can reveal more supporting evidence for
these speculations and new information for other
hypotheses. By continued concentration on the
fossil record, in particular fossil flowers, the
mystery of the origin and evolution of angiosperms can ultimately be resolved.

Appendix

Table showing sequence of ages of the Cretaceous period (Hughes 1976b, fig. 7.1).

Era	Period	Age	Million years
Mesozoic	Cretaceous	Maestrichtian	65 ± 2
		Campanian	
		Santonian	
		Coniacian	
		Turonian	
		Cenomanian	(100)
		Albian	
		Aptian	
		Barremian	
		Hauterivian	
		Valanginian	
		Berriasian	135 ± 5

Fossil Flowers

12

References

Basinger, J. F.; Dilcher, D. L. Ancient bisexual
    flowers. Science 224:511-513; 1984.

Beck, C. B. Origin and early evolution of angio-
    sperms: a perspective. In: Beck, C. B., ed.
    Origin and early evolution of angiosperms.
    New York: Columbia University Press;
    1976:1-10.

Crepet, W. L. Ancient flowers for the faithful.
    Nat. Hist. 1984 April:39-44.

Cronquist, A. The evolution and classification
    of flowering plants. Riverside Studies in
    Biology. Boston: Houghton Mifflin; 1968.

Dilcher, D. L.; Crane, P. R. In pursuit of the
    first flower. Natural History. March:57-60.

Dilcher, D. L.; Crepet, W. L.; Beeker, C. D.;
    Reynolds, H. C. Reproductive and vegetative
    morphology of a Cretaceous angiosperm.
    Science 191:854-856; 1976.

Friis, E. M.; Sharby A. Scandianthus gen. nov.,
    angiosperm flowers of saxifragalean
    affinity from the Upper Cretaceous of
    southern Sweden. Ann. of Bot. 50:569-583;
    1982.

Hughes, N. F. Cretaceous paleobotanic problems.
    In: Beck, C. B., ed. Origin and early
    evolution of angiosperms. New York:
    Columbia University Press; 1976a:11-22.

Fossil Flowers

13

Hughes, N. F. Paleobiology of angiosperm
    origins: problems of Mesozoic seed-plant
    evolution. Cambridge Earth Science Series.
    London: Cambridge University Press; 1976b.
Tiffney, B. H. Dicotyledonous angiosperm flower
    from the Upper Cretaceous of Martha's
    Vineyard, Massachusetts. Nature
    265:136-137; 1977.

SAMPLE
SCIENCE PAPER—LAB REPORT

CH 221/222   Name: J. Stone, R. Smith

Prof. J. Burke   Date: 02-16-92

LABORATORY REPORT FORM

Experiment No. and Title:

#7: Synthesis of Ethyl B-Naptholate (Nerolin)

References:

Miller & Neuzil, Modern Experimental Organic Chemistry, D.C. Heath, 1982

Description:

To a solution of potassium hydroxide (4.0 g; 0.09 m) in absolute methanol (50 mL) was added b-naphthol (5.0 g; 0.35 m), followed by ethyl iodide (3 mL; 0.037 m). After refluxing for 2 hours, the mixture was poured over cracked ice (150 mL) and stirred thoroughly. A white precipitate was collected by vacuum filtration and washed with water (ca., 20 mL) afforded white needles 1.26 g, Mp 35-36 C; Lit. Mp 35.5-35C). IR and NMR were not obtained.

Results/Yield:

1.26g/172.23g/m = 0.00073 mole obtained. 0.035 mole theory (from B=naphthol). 0.00073/0.035 = 0.209 = 21% Yield.

Conclusion

Based on sharpness of melting point range and its close agreement with the literature value, the product appears to be quite pure.

1. Miller & Neuzil (above reference).

WRITING IN
BUSINESS

Business writing involves correspondence and reports. Its purpose is to inform business associates, vendors, customers, and other interested parties what is being or has been done and to persuade them to do something. Various types of business correspondence and reports follow specific prescribed formats. The text within these formats may develop inductively or deductively, depending on the purpose of the document.

RESEARCH SOURCES

Information for reports may come from either primary or secondary research. Sometimes primary research is conducted to determine what resources are available, what other businesses are doing, or what changes are occurring in the marketplace. This research may take the form of interviews, surveys, observation, or analysis of internal records. Sometimes library searches are used to determine economic conditions, competition, changing demographics, technology, or historical events.

The resources available for library searches are extensive. Some are more highly specialized than undergraduates need. Some deal with only one product. Some are available in print, on CD-ROM, and on-line. Some are available only on-line, especially the most specialized ones. Some on-line sources are updated as frequently as every 15 minutes. Some are very expensive—more than $100 per connect hour.

Because undergraduates will find that less specialized resources will meet most of their needs, they should concentrate on resources that focus on descriptions of markets of companies, reports of their performances, and comparisons of companies to other companies. Some of those resources will be indexes that lead to abstracts and articles in journals.

The following references will give the business student some resources with which to start. They are appropriate for students studying accounting, advertising, computer information systems, finance, management, marketing, and other areas of business.

SPECIALIZED LIBRARY SOURCES

The following references will provide useful information on the general background of companies: history, officers, products, profits, projections, markets, and competition.

Periodical and Newspaper Indexes

Much current information about companies, markets, and economic conditions appears in periodicals and newspapers and can be located by using indexes like those listed below.

> *Reader's Guide to Periodical Literature*
> *Business Periodicals Index*
> *Wall Street Journal Index*
> *New York Times Index*
> *Social Sciences Index*
> Predicast's *F & S Index of Corporations and Industries*

If you cannot find the journal or newspaper to which one of these indexes refers you, you should see the reference librarian. Most academic libraries are members of an interlibrary loan association and can obtain materials from other libraries. This service is generally free.

You can use CD-ROM (Compact Disk-Read Only Memory) to search the *Business Periodicals Index, Social Sciences Index,* and five other databases. Networked workstations permit menu-driven searching with printouts of search results. Cited journals are usually tagged to indicate the library's holdings.

Another alternative is to use the library's usually free computerized literature search service. This allows you to do the equivalent of a periodical index search on your research topic using Dialog's database. This index will give you a list of periodical articles on your exact topic. You will then have to find the actual articles in the library from the periodicals section (listed alphabetically) or from the interlibrary loan service. See your reference librarian for assistance on computerized literature search.

Economic Indicators
These monthly periodicals give information on twelve leading economic indicators.

U.S. Government Publications
These monthly publications yield valuable demographic and statistical information.

> *Standard Industrial Classification Manual (SIC)*
> *Economic Censuses* (every five years)
> *Survey of Current Business* (monthly in periodicals)
> *Business Statistics* (biennial)
> *U.S. Industrial Outlook*
> *The Encyclopedia of Associations* (annual, multivolume)
> *Dun and Bradstreet's Industry Norm and Key Business Ratios*
> *Standard and Poor's Industry Surveys*
> *Moody's Industry Review*
> "Annual Report on American Industry" in *Forbes* magazine
>   (January issue)
> *Standard Directory of Advertising Agencies*
> *U.S. Census*

Marketing Guides and Atlas

> *Sales and Marketing Management Survey of Buying Power*
>   *(S&MM)*
> *Editor and Publisher Market Guide*
> *Rand McNally Commercial Atlas*

Corporate Annual Reports
Current reports for many corporations are available on microfiche in libraries or from the company's public affairs office.

Directories and Registers

Corporate addresses and basic operating information can be obtained from directories and registers.

> *Standard and Poor's Register of Corporations*
> *Moody Industrial Manual*
> *Million Dollar Directory*
> *Macmillan Directory of Leading Private Companies*
> *Thomas Register on American Manufacturers*
> *Dun and Bradstreet "Million Dollar Directory"*
> *Standard Directory of Advertisers*
> *Trade Names Dictionary*
> *Everybody's Business*
> *Marketing Studies*

SPECIALIZED DATABASES FOR COMPUTER SEARCHES

> *ACM—Computer Archive (CD-ROM)*
> *Compact Disclosure*
> *ABI/Inform*
> *Business Software Database*
> *The Computer Database*
> *Microcomputer Index*
> *Microcomputer Software and Hardware Guide*

NON-LIBRARY SOURCES

Much research for business is conducted by sorting through company records; interviewing, questioning, and surveying appropriate people; observing performance and production; and writing to various government departments and bureaus. Some of these are the U.S. Bureau of Industrial Economics, the Industry Publications Division, Trade Development, the U.S. Bureau of Census, and the U.S. Department of Commerce. Company annual reports can be obtained by writing directly to the company, and additional information can be obtained about a small company by writing to or calling local newspapers in the town in which the company is located.

ASSIGNMENTS IN BUSINESS WRITING

Writing assignments in business writing class ask students to use specific formats for memos, letters, and reports.

MEMOS AND LETTERS

Memos are used to communicate with associates within the organization. Letters are used to communicate with associates, clients, and customers outside the organization. The messages of memos and letters can be divided roughly into three types: pleasant, unpleasant, and persuasive. Pleasant ones are usually developed deductively; that is, the main message is stated first, details about the main message are related in the second paragraph, and socially appropriate comments bring the message to a conclusion. Usually, the active voice is used for pleasant messages.

Unpleasant and persuasive messages are usually developed inductively; that is, the writer tries to establish rapport in the first paragraph, introduce the topic in the second, relate the unpleasant message or request in the third or fourth, and close on common ground in the last. Frequently, the passive voice is used to distance the writer from the unpleasant messages.

The tone of a memo or letter depends on the relationship between the writer and the intended reader, the purpose of the message, and the expected attitude of the intended reader to the message.

REPORTS

Reports take a variety of forms determined by their purpose. Some are informational, some are analytical, and some are persuasive. Annual, procedural, and progress reports convey information. Evaluation reports analyze and pass judgment. Justification and recommendation reports and proposals aim to persuade.

One type of specialized report is the marketing plan. It follows a format similar to the marketing planning outline below.

Strategic Marketing Planning Outline

  I. Executive Summary
 II. The Business Opportunity
     A. The Core Product/Service Concept
III. Situation Analysis
     A. Organizational Mission, Goals, and Objectives
     B. Resources Required
 IV. Marketing Action Plan
     A. Overview of the Industry
     B. Macro Environmental Factors
     C. Organizational Strengths/Weaknesses
     D. Competitors' Strengths/Weaknesses
     E. Marketing Goals and Objectives
     F. Marketing Research Results/Recommendations
     G. Market Segmentation
     H. Target Market Selection
     I. Product Positioning
  V. Marketing Mix Strategy
     A. Product Definition
     B. Pricing Strategy
     C. Promotional Strategy
     D. Distribution Strategy
 VI. Implementation
     A. Action Plan
     B. Functional Responsibilities
     C. Financial Assumptions
     D. Demand Forecasts
     E. Pro Forma Analysis
VII. Controls
VIII. Risk Assessment

CONVENTIONS OF STYLE AND FORMAT

Because time is money for both the writer and the reader, business writing is clear and concise. Memos and letters do not take more than one page without a good reason.

Every part of a business document, conveys a message: the paper, the letterhead, the print, the placement on the page, the organization, the words and phrasing of the message, and the spelling and punctuation. High-quality stationery and print says that the business is prosperous and that the sender may have a high position in the organization. Aesthetically pleasing placement of type on the page and well-chosen words and flawless mechanics convey an image of competence and are expected in all business correspondence. A client receiving a letter from an accountant with errors in spelling or punctuation may begin to question the accuracy of the accountant's figures.

Paragraphs and sentences in business memos are usually kept short. Although the purpose and intended reader determine the length of both, between four and eight lines is recommended. Frequently, a paragraph in a letter or memo may have only one or two sentences. Because reading difficulty is determined by length of sentences and number of difficult words (words of three or more syllables according to the Gunning-Fog Index), sentences should be kept under 20 words in length.

When important information can be listed, it is usually listed with each item preceded by a bullet, dash, asterisk, or numeral. This format enables the reader to find the information quickly on the first reading and again when using the letter for reference or responding.

MEMOS AND LETTERS

Because memos travel within an organization, they have a simple heading which is frequently printed for use by the company. This heading includes the following components:

To:

From:

Date:

Re:

Although the order of these items may vary, the items themselves are standard. They are placed about an inch from the top of the page or two spaces below the letterhead if letterhead paper is used. Because a memo's message begins two or three spaces below its heading, the memo usually does not look centered on the page.

A business letter should look centered on the page, slightly higher rather than lower. The lines of paragraphs should be single-spaced—with double-spacing between paragraphs. The first word of each paragraph may be indented, but the trend is to start each line at the left margin. Other trends are as follows:

- To omit *dear* in the salutation when the writer does not know the reader

- To omit the salutation and complimentary close if the name of the reader is not known

- To use *attention* and *subject* lines especially when the salutation is being omitted

Remember, time is money. Businesses want to save time in both producing and reading correspondence. Aesthetic appeal communicates prosperity and competence. Do not underestimate the importance of either in writing for business.

REPORTS

A report may be considered formal or informal depending on the number of supplementary parts, which tend to increase as the length of the body of the report increases. A formal report may have a cover; title fly sheet; title page; table of contents; table of figures; letter of transmittal; glossary; endnotes, works cited, or references; and appendices.

- The **title fly** is a blank sheet of paper placed between the cover and title page in the most formal reports.

- The **title page** gives the title, name(s) of the intended reader(s), name(s) of the sender(s), and date of completion.

- The **table of contents** lists the internal headings of the body of the report and the supplementary parts in the order in which they appear and the numbers of the pages on which they begin.

- The **letter of transmittal** addresses the intended reader, the person who authorized the production of the report. It responds to the letter of authorization and tells what the writers did and how they did it.

- The **summary** contains the main points of the report in less than a page. Some departments, such as engineering, like them even shorter. If readers being addressed by the document are in higher management, the summary is called an "Executive Summary." Summaries of highly technical reports are frequently written in lay language.

- The **body** typically introduces its parts with internal headings. The subjects and order of these parts are determined pragmatically. However, the most important facts usually come first to save time for the reader.

- The **glossary** defines any words that some of the intended readers may need to have defined.

- The **appendix** includes any supporting materials that are referenced in the text: tables, charts, graphs, contracts, photographs, maps, floor plans, graphic illustrations, graphic exhibits, questionnaires, and pictures. Each item in an appendix should have a title. A report may have more than one appendix when need demands more.

Students writing business reports commonly feel uncomfortable with the overlapping of information in the letter of transmittal, the summary, and the introduction and conclusion of the body. True, these parts overlap, but each is there for a different purpose and a different intended reader. Some readers need to be familiar with the general scope of the report but do not have to know the details. They read the summary only. Other readers must know the details. They read the whole report. In highly technical reports that must be read by managers who do not know the technical language, summaries are written in language appropriate for these readers.

DOCUMENTATION FORMATS

Because many institutions and industrial organizations publish their own documentation manuals, styles may vary in this discipline more than in the others discussed in this book. If the employer specifies an in-house or other style, the writer must follow it. However, if no style is specified, the writer may choose from a number of recommended styles, such as MLA, APA, or Chicago style.

In any case, information is cited in the text, in footnotes, in endnotes, or in works cited or reference supplements in accordance with the chosen style.

SAMPLE STUDENT PAPERS IN BUSINESS

Two student reports follow: an analysis and a proposal. The analysis draws from secondary research and uses the MLA format. The proposal relies on primary research which is documented in the text.

An Analysis of
the Growth Potential of
Candela Laser Corporation

for

Dr. Richard Maxell
Bay State Eye and Health Care
Weymouth, Massachusetts

by

Janet Sheehan
Financial Consultant
ABC Financial Consultants

November 4, 1988

ii

Bay State Eye and Health Care
320 Washington Street
Suite 205
Weymouth, MA 02186
September 30, 1988

Janet Sheehan
ABC Financial Consultants
500 River Street
Braintree, MA 02184

Dear Ms. Sheehan:

I would like you to prepare a report about Candela Laser Corporation that will assist me in my decision to buy stock.

I would like you to research the financial statements of 1987 and 1988.

Specifically, I would like you to research the growth potential of Candela Laser Corporation and recommend whether or not to make an investment.

As you know, Candela Laser Corporation is planning a public stock offering on November 15, 1988. From the outside, Candela appears to have an excellent growth potential. But we all know that every good investment decision is backed by hours of research on the inside operations of a corporation. I will base my decision on your report and recommendation.

You can call me at (617) 337-1234 to discuss your fees. Please have this report in my office by November 5, 1988.

Sincerely,

Richard Maxell, Ph. D.

iii

ABC Financial Consultants
500 River Street
Braintree, MA 02184
November 4, 1988

Dr. Richard Maxell
Bay State Eye and Health Care
Suite 205
Weymouth, MA 02186

Dear Dr. Maxell:

Here is the report about Candela Laser Corporation that you requested.

The report focuses on the growth potential of
Candela Laser Corporation based on an analysis
of the 1987 and 1988 financial statements.

After extensive research on the above financial
statements, I have concluded that Candela Laser
Corporation is violating Statement of Financial
Accounting Standards 48 which deals with revenue
recognition. This raises the question of whether
or not Candela Laser Corporation can continue
doing business. I recommend that you do not
participate in Candela Laser Corporation's
public stock offering.

If you have any questions, please do not hesi-
tate to call me at (617) 843-1234, extension 21.

Sincerely,

Janet Sheehan

Janet Sheehan

iv

CONTENTS

v

Summary

   Candela Laser Corporation began by developing scientific lasers and now develops dermatology and urology lasers as well.

   Candela tripled its sales in one quarter
and turned its loss of $1.3 million into a
profit of $727,000 in one year, due to its sales
of dermatology and urology lasers. But while
doing so, it violated Statement of Financial
Accounting Standards 48, "Revenue Recognition
When Right of Return Exists."

   The result of that violation decreases the
1988 reported profit of $727,000 to a loss of
almost $2 million.

   Due to high marketing and developing costs
associated with this industry and the loss in
1988, Candela Laser Corporation may not be able
to continue doing business in the future. Therefore I recommend that you do not participate in
the November 15, 1988, public stock offering.

1

INTRODUCTION

Candela Laser Corporation was founded in
1970 by two physicists, Horace Furumoto and
Harry Ceccon. From 1970 to 1980, Candela Laser
Corporation developed scientific lasers and sold
them to universities and federal agencies. Sales
were less than $1 million per year.

In 1981, Candela began to develop dermatology and urology lasers. To market the lasers,
Candela raised $4.2 million in a June, 1986,
public stock offering at $3 per share. Late in
1986, Candela began to market both lasers. In
April of 1987, Candela began to ship its urology
laser. In June 1987, Candela raised another $5
million in a private offering of their stock. In
March, 1988, Candela shipped its dermatology
laser. By June 30, 1988, medical laser systems
accounted for 68% of Candela's sales. According
to Richard J. Olsen, the chief financial
officer, Candela believes that its dermatology
laser alone will bring in $60 million over the
next five years (Fitz Simon 38).

In April, 1988, Candela received The New
Englander Award, issued annually by the Small
Business Association of New England, Inc. (Fitz
Simon 38).

Candela is already researching developing
lasers to treat eye diseases and to blast plaque
from clogged arteries (Fitz Simon 38).

2

THE PROBLEM

Financial Statement Analysis

As Figure 1 shows, in the first three quarters of the year ended June 30, 1987, Candela suffered losses due to high marketing costs. Then in the last quarter, as Candela began to ship its urology laser, sales almost tripled, resulting in a profit of $108,000. But overall, for the year ended June 30, 1987, Candela suffered a loss of $1.3 million.

For the year ended June 30, 1988, the year during which Candela began shipping its dermatology laser, Candela reported a profit of $727,830.

Figure 1
Candela's Condensed Financial Statements (000)

quarter ended---	9/30/86	12/31/86	3/31/87	6/30/87	Total
sales	$ 843	$ 799	$1,010	$2,900	$5,552
expenses	1,051	1,903	1,644	2,792	6,890
profit/ (loss)	$ (208)	$ (604)	$ (634)	$ 108	$(1,338)

quarter ended---	9/30/87	12/31/87	3/31/88	6/30/88	Total
sales	$2,800	$3,100	$3,910	$5,970	$15,780
expenses	2,642	3,264	3,758	5,389	15,053
profit/ (loss)	$ 158	$ (164)	$ 152	$ 581	$ 727

Source: Wall Street Journal Quarterly Earnings Digest

3

It is very unusual for any company to turn a $1.3 million loss into a $727,000 profit in one year. After further analysis of the notes to the financial statements, specifically the one cited in Exhibit 1, I have found that Candela is violating the revenue recognition policy, resulting in incorrect sales figures and an overstatement of income.

Revenue Recognition

The basic concept of revenue recognition is to recognize revenue when it is earned, realized, and recognizable, or, when the product is substantially completed and shipped to the customer. Candela Laser Corporation completed its lasers and shipped them to their customers, justifying revenue recognition according to the basic concept as shown in Exhibit 1. But many of Candela's "customers" included independent distributors who had the right to return the lasers (Fitz Simon 71). A sale with the right to return is one of the exceptions to the basic concept.

Candela has violated SFAS 48, "Revenue Recognition When Right of Return Exists." Candela had sold many of its lasers to independent distributors who retained the right to return the lasers if they were unable to sell to hospitals, clinics, or doctors.

Under SFAS 48, six requirements must be met in order to count the sale as revenue at the point of sale. The six requirements are shown in Exhibit 2. If not all the requirements are met, revenue cannot be recognized until the right to return provision expires.

4

One of the requirements is that the buyer,
the independent distributors in this case, is
indebted to the seller and the indebtedness is
not contingent on the resale of the merchandise.
Candela has stated that payment from the distributors is dependent on the resale of the
system (Fitz Simon 71). Therefore, Candela does
not meet this requirement.

Another requirement is that a reasonable
estimate can be made of future returns that will
be allowed. According to Martin Miller, author
of GAAP Guide, SFAS 48 cites the following
factors that decrease the possibility of making
a reasonable estimate:

1. Possible technical obsolescence or change in
    demand for merchandise
2. Little or no experience in determining
    returns for specific types of merchandise

Laser technology is a rapidly changing technology. Therefore, technical obsolescence is
possible. As a matter of fact, another one of
Candela's problems is that it had technically
obsolete inventory. This would lead to decreasing the possibility of making a reasonable
estimate. Also, medical lasers are fairly new
technology. Candela has not had the experience
required to determine an estimate of the
returns. Candela has not met the requirement of
making a reasonable estimate of future returns.

5

CONCLUSION

Although laser technology has a promising future, that future is not with Candela Laser Corporation.

After analyzing revenue transactions more carefully, I have concluded that since Candela did not meet the requirements of SFAS 48, Candela could not report certain sales as revenues. The sales that Candela should not have reported amount to approximately $2.7 million in 1988. This would have left Candela suffering a loss of about $2 million instead of a profit of $727,000 in 1988. This restatement is shown in Figure 2. Because of the high marketing and developing costs that any company in the medical laser field must face, I have serious doubts that Candela can continue doing business in the future. Therefore I recommend that you do not participate in the November 15, 1988, public stock offering.

Figure 2
Candela's 1988 Financial Statement Restated (000)

sales	$13,080
expenses	15,053
	--------
profit/(loss)	$(1,973)
	========

6

Exhibit 1

Candela Laser Corporation

Excerpts from Notes to Financial Statements

For Year Ended June 30, 1987

Revenue Recognition:

    Generally, the Company recognizes revenue as completed machines are shipped to customers.

7

Exhibit 2
Summary of the Provisions of SFAS 48

When a buyer has the right to return merchandise purchased, the seller may not recognize income from the sale, unless all of the following conditions are met:

1. The price between the seller and the buyer is substantially fixed, or determinable.

2. The seller has received full payment, or the buyer is indebted to the seller and the indebtedness is not contingent on the resale of the merchandise.

3. Physical destruction, damage, or theft of the merchandise would not change the buyer's obligation to the seller.

4. The buyer has economic substance and does not exist solely for the benefit of the seller.

5. No significant obligations exist for the seller to help the buyer resell the merchandise.

6. A reasonable estimate can be made of the amount of future returns.

8

Works Cited

Fitz Simon, Jane. "Lasers Glow Like Gold at
    Candela." The Boston Globe, 10 May 1988:
    33+.

---. "Audit Problem Stops Candela's Public
    Offering." The Boston Globe, 2 November
    1988: 71+

Miller, Martin. GAAP Guide. New York: HBJ, 1990.

Proposal:

Raising Telephone Rates at

The City View Hotel

Nicole Gallant

Prof. Polanski

Writing for Business

April 28, 1992

ii

Mr. Michael da Silva
City View Hotel
104 Lobster Lane
Bayview, SC 04596

April 16, 1992

Dear Michael:

Here is the report about raising the current
telephone charges at the City View Hotel. I surveyed several of the local Bayview hotels and
discovered that the City View charges lower
rates in the following areas:

1. Local calls
2. Long distance markup
3. 1-800 calls
4. Directory assistance
5. Pay stations

Based on these results I propose the following
increases:

1. Local calls by $.15
2. Long distance markup by 9.4%
3. 1-800 calls by $.75
4. Directory assistance by $.15
5. Pay stations by 20%

These proposed increases would significantly
increase telephone revenue. Hotel profit would
rise by an estimated $108,666.00 annually. This
is a great way for the hotel to earn a larger
profit. This added profit would allow the hotel
to improve the current services offered to
guests and to find more ways to satisfy guest
and employee needs.

As you requested, a copy of this report was sent
to Mr. Alan and Mr. Michael Spaulding.

Sincerely,

Nicole Gallant

Nicole Gallant

iii

Ms. Nicole Gallant
City View Hotel
104 Lobster Lane
Bayview, SC 04596

March 16, 1992

Dear Nicole:

Please write a report proposing an increase in
the hotel's current telephone charges. It has
come to my attention that the City View Hotel
charges the guests below average rates for
local, long distance and credit card calls. An
increase in these charges could be very
profitable for the hotel.

This report should include the average rate
charged to guests by local Bayview hotels, an
estimate of increase needed to bring rates to
the average, and graphs showing the forecasted
profit that will result from an increase.

Please finish this report by April 16, 1992.
Send copies of the finished report to the hotel
owners Mr. Alan and Mr. Michael Spaulding. Thank
you for your time and help.

Sincerely,

Michael da Silva

Michael da Silva

iv

TABLE OF CONTENTS

v

TABLE OF FIGURES

vi

EXECUTIVE SUMMARY

The City View Hotel charges below average telephone rates. This report proposes increases in
the following areas:

1. Local calls
2. Long distance markup
3. 1-800 calls
4. Directory assistance
5. Pay stations

These increases would help the hotel generate an
estimated profit of $807,415 annually. This
would mean that there would be an increase in
current telephone revenue of $108,666. These
figures are based on the average number of calls
made by hotel guests during the past year.

INTRODUCTION

One way for the City View Hotel to compete
better with local hotels is to raise telephone
rates. Currently the City View charges telephone
rates that are below the average charged by the
surrounding hotels.

Increasing the telephone rates at the City View
to meet the average of the local hotels will
mean a greater revenue. This increased revenue
will allow the hotel to spend more money on
improving guest services. This would ensure
guest satisfaction, return visits, and a better
all-around reputation for the City View. This
would also increase hotel revenue because guests
would return to the hotel and recommend the City
View to their friends and business associates.

SURVEY

Hotels surveyed:
Ten local Bayview hotels were surveyed in order
to prepare this report. Following is a list of
the hotels that were involved in the survey.

1. City View Hotel
2. Seaview Inn
3. Hill Crest Hotel
4. Drop Inn
5. Bay Towers

6. Edelweiss Lodge
7. Fieldbrook House
8. The White Hart
9. The Castle
10. The Gatehouse

Method:
A call-around was conducted to survey the hotels
listed above. I called each of these hotels and
spoke with the Communications Manager or the
Front Desk Manager. Some of the smaller hotels
did not have a specific Communications Manager.

I questioned each manager about his or her
telephone charges in each of the following
areas:

1. Local calls
2. Long distance markup
3. Access charge for credit cards
4. 1-800 calls
5. 1-900, 1-950, & 1-550 calls
6. Directory assistance
7. Pay stations

3

Results:

Figure 1

TELEPHONE CHARGE SURVEY

	City View Hotel	Seaview Inn	Hill Crest Hotel	Drop Inn	Bay Towers
Local calls	$.60	$.75	$.75	$.60	$.90
Long distance markup	32%	30%	38%	35%	--
Access charge credit cards	$.75	$.75	$.75	$.65	--
1-800 calls	$.00	$.00	$.75	$.00	--
1-900, 1-950, 1-550 calls	NO	NO	NO	NO	--
Pay stations	14%	20%	25%	20%	--
Directory assistance	$.60 local $.75 long distance	$.75	$.75	$.75	--

	Edelweiss Lodge	Fieldbrook House	The White Hart	The Castle	The Gate-house
Local calls	$.80	$.60	$.90	$.75	$.85
Long distance markup	92%	35%	99%	40%	50%
Access charge credit cards	$.92	$.75	$1.00	$1.00	$.00
1-800 calls	$.92	$.75	$.90	$.75	$.00
1-900, 1-950, 1-550 calls	NO	NO	NO	YES $5.00	NO
Pay stations	15%	20%	25%	20%	20%
Directory assistance	$.92	$.60	$.50	$.75	$.85

4

Problems with the survey:

The Bay Towers refused to participate in the
whole survey and answered only the first
question. The manager said it was illegal for
them to give out the hotel charges for telephone
rates. After talking with several of our managers and law consultants, I verified that the
Bay Towers was incorrect. It is not illegal for
hotels to disclose their telephone charges to
outside sources or guests. If a guest disputes a
bill, that guest has a right to know what he is
being charged for. The Bay Towers is one of the
most expensive and exclusive hotels in the city;
they probably want to maintain this image by
refusing to participate in this survey.

Discussion of results:

1. Local calls
The City View charges $.60 for local calls. On
the average this is $.15 less than the sur-
rounding Bayview hotels. The range of charges
for this fee is from $.60 to $.90. The City View
falls at the very bottom of the scale.

2. Long distance markup
The City View also falls at the bottom of the
scale in this category. Our hotel currently
marks up long distance phone calls by 32%. This
is three points less than the two other
Spaulding hotels. The more expensive hotels,
like the Bay Towers and The White Hart, affected

5

the average because their markups are 90%-99%.
The average for the local hotels that fall in
the same price range as the City View is 39%.

3. Access charge for credit cards
All the hotels surveyed, except The Gatehouse,
charge a fee for using credit cards. The average
for this fee is $.73. The City View is above
average by $.02.

4. 1-800 calls
Through this survey it was discovered that the
local hotels are beginning to charge a hook-up
fee for 1-800 phone calls. The majority of the
hotels that charge for this service use the same
amount for this fee as they do for local calls.
This is due to the fact that the hook-up fee
charged to the hotel by the phone company for
1-800 calls is the same as that for local calls.
If the hotels do not charge the guests for these
calls, they will lose money because they are
still responsible for paying the phone company.
The hotels that already charge for this service
have seen an increase in revenue. The average
for this fee is $.81 and the City View currently
falls way below average because it does not
charge for this service.

5. 1-900, 1-950, 1-550 calls
Of all the hotels surveyed, only The Castle
allows 1-900 calls to be made from the guest
rooms. The Castle charges $5.00 for these calls.

6

The City View falls in line with the other
hotels by restricting 1-900 calls. This restriction means that guests are not allowed to make
1-900 calls from their rooms.

6. Pay stations
The average markup for pay stations is 20%. This
puts the City View below average by 6 points
because the current markup is 14%.

7. Directory assistance
Through this survey it was discovered that the
City View is the only hotel that charges
different rates for local and long distance
directory assistance. The City View charges $.60
for local directory assistance and $.75 for long
distance directory assistance. The average for
this fee is $.71. The City view is below average
for local calls and above average for long
distance calls.

PROPOSED INCREASES
As a result of this survey, I propose that the
hotel increase its telephone charges in the
following areas:

1. Local calls
2. Directory assistance
3. 1-800 calls
4. Long distance markup
5. Pay stations

7

Local calls: (see figure 2)
This fee should be raised by $.15 in order for
our prices to meet the average of the local
Bayview hotels.

Directory assistance: (see figure 2)
This fee should be consistent for local and long
distance directory assistance. This consistency
can be created by increasing the charge for
local directory assistance to $.75. By
increasing this charge, the three Spaulding
hotels will have uniformed rates.

1-800 calls: (see figure 2)
Since most hotels in this area are beginning to
charge for 1-800 calls, I propose that the City
View also instate this fee. It would be
appropriate to charge $.75 for this service
because $.75 will cover the cost of connecting
the guest to an outside line.

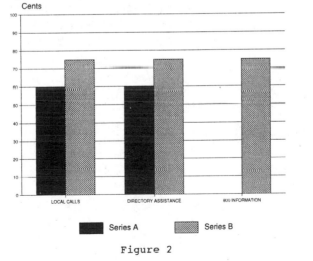

Figure 2

8

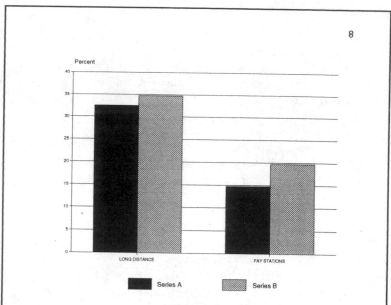

Figure 3

Long distance markup: (see figure 3)
I propose that the City View raise its markup to
35% in order to unify the three Spaulding hotels
and have them all charge the same rate. This
will also bring the City View closer to the
average rate.

Pay stations: (see figure 3)
The markup for the pay stations at the City View
is currently below average. I propose that this
percentage be raised to 20% in order for the
hotel to measure up with the going rates.

9

FORECASTED PROFIT FOR EACH INCREASE

The following forecasted increases are based on
the number of calls made from the City View
Hotel last year.

Local calls:
With an increase of $.15 for local calls the
hotel will earn a net increase of $28,908.75.

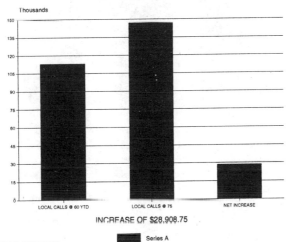

Figure 4

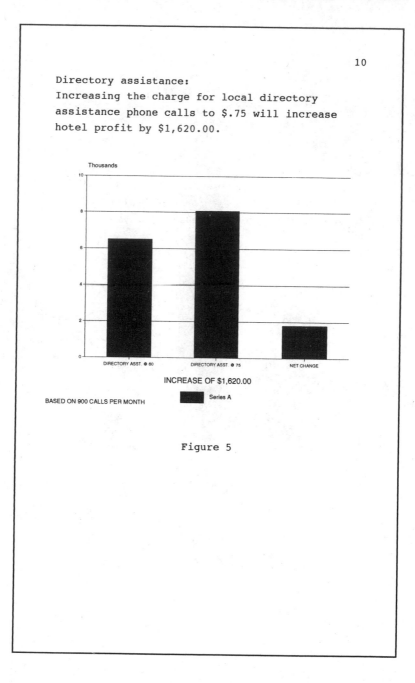

10

Directory assistance:
Increasing the charge for local directory
assistance phone calls to $.75 will increase
hotel profit by $1,620.00.

Thousands

INCREASE OF $1,620.00

BASED ON 900 CALLS PER MONTH   Series A

DIRECTORY ASST. @ 60   DIRECTORY ASST. @ 75   NET CHANGE

Figure 5

11

1-800 calls:
Instating a new charge of $.75 for 1-800 calls will
increase hotel profit by $13,500.00.

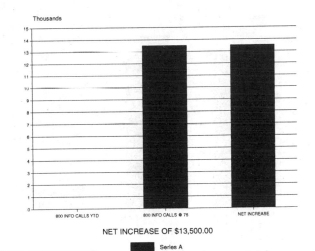

Thousands

NET INCREASE OF $13,500.00

BASED ON 1500 CALLS PER MONTH

Series A

Figure 6

12

Long distance markup:
By increasing the long distance markup to 35%
the hotel will earn a net increase of
$52,675.22.

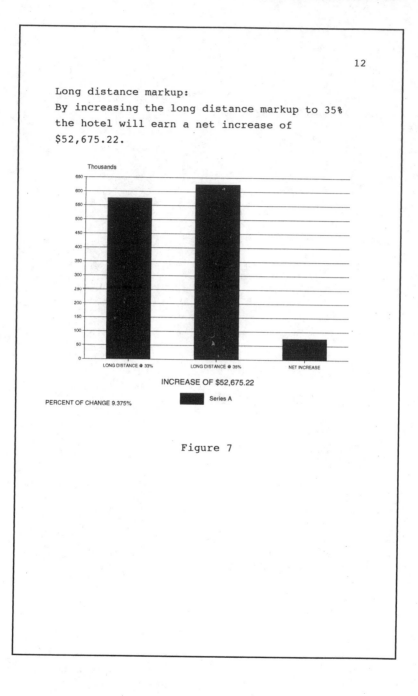

INCREASE OF $52,675.22

PERCENT OF CHANGE 9.375%

Figure 7

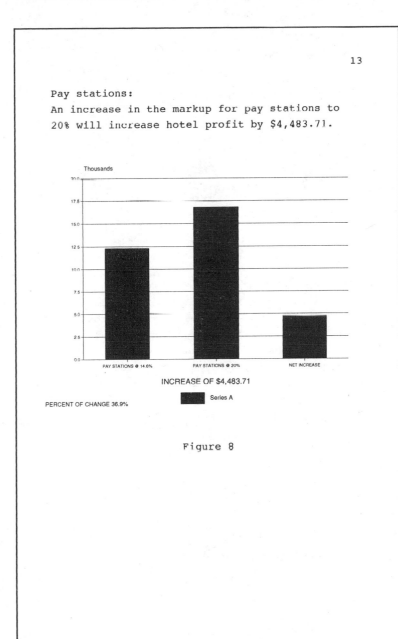

Figure 8

14

FORECASTED REVENUE

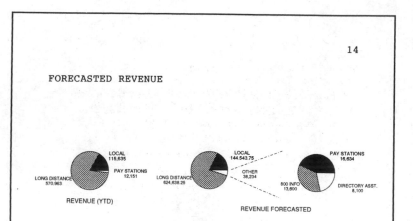

Figure 9

The telephone revenue year to date is equal to
$698,749.00, which is a good amount for the size
of this hotel. However, these slight increases
in rates will greatly increase annual revenue by
$108,666.00. Based on the number of phone calls
made by guests last year, this will mean an
estimated annual revenue of $807,415.00.

15

BENEFITS OF THESE INCREASES

As a result of these increases, the City View
will receive many benefits. First and most
important is the increase in hotel revenue. With
this new revenue the hotel will have an opportunity to satisfy guests and employee needs more
efficiently. There are many areas where this
money could be used to improve the hotel. The
money will not pay for all of these, but the
suggestions are as follows:

1. Renovate the guest rooms. The monthly comment
cards reveal that the guests are dissatisfied
with the noise level of the hotel and the heating units. This extra money could be used to
discover ways to soundproof the rooms. Because
the City View is such an old hotel, the heating
system is also very old. This money could be put
to updating this system so that the guest rooms
are not extremely hot or cold. This would make
the guests happier, improve the comments on the
comment cards, and make guests more willing to
return to the hotel and recommend this hotel to
their friends.

2. Hire more bellmen. Lack of bellmen is another
common complaint on the comment cards. Due to
the economy the City View has had to cut back on
help. This added revenue could be used to invest
in more bellmen. This would make check-in go
smoother and faster. The guests would be happier
because they would have quicker service getting
to their room and the guest service agents would
be happier because they would not have to listen

16

to guests yell at them as a result of a short
bell staff. Comment cards would also improve
because guests would be happier.

3. Create more hotel advertisements. By spending
more money on advertising the name and reputation of our hotel would reach more people world-
wide. This will attract more travelers and also
increase hotel profit. The more a person hears
the name of a hotel the more interested he or
she is to stay at the hotel.

4. Buy new uniforms for hotel employees. This
would please employees by giving them a little
extra boost and it may make them happier with
their job to know that they are being thought of
by the management.

5. Give raises to hard-working hotel employees.
There are many dedicated employees who are
becoming dissatisfied with the hotel because
they are not receiving the appreciation that
they deserve.

6. Set up a day-care service for employees and
guests. This would make life easier for the
employees who have small children and find it
difficult to work and raise a family. This
service could also be offered to guests
traveling with children who may want to go out
for a night on the town and to leave the little
ones at home.

7. Set up a service for employees with the surrounding garages which would allow employees to park in a garage for a lower rate. This would make an easier and more pleasant commute for many employees who have difficulty using public transportation due to their work schedules.

OVERVIEW OF
DOCUMENTATION STYLES: BOOKS

MLA Format (pp. 42–59)

Parenthetical citation in the text

> ... Thoreau's reference to Abraham Lincoln (Miller 308).

Work cited at the end of the paper

> Miller, Perry. The American Transcendentalists: Their Prose and Poetry. New York: Doubleday, 1983.

Chicago Format (pp. 59–64)

Note in the text

> ... acknowledged in 1902 with the Hay-Pauncefote Treaties.[1]

Work listed at the end of the paper

Notes:
> 1. David Weigall, Britain and the World: 1815-1986 (New York: Oxford University Press, 1987), 107.

Bibliography:
> Weigall, David. Britain and the World: 1815-1986. New York: Oxford University Press, 1987.

APA Format (pp. 114–122)

Parenthetical citation in the text
> ... a psychological profile of Adolph Hitler (Langer, 1972).

Reference at the end of the paper
```
      Langer, W. C. (1972). The mind of Adolph
Hitler. New York: Basic.
```

CBE Number-Reference Format (See sample paper, p. 175–188)

Parenthetical citation in the text
```
... against a living snail has been documented
(1, p. 432).
```

Reference at the end of the paper
```
   1. Barth, R. H.; Broshears, R. E. The
      invertebrate world. Philadelphia: Saunders
      College Publishing; 1982.
```

Author–Date Format (See sample paper, p. 191–204)

Parenthetical citation in the text
```
... know where and when angiosperms arose
(Hughes 1976b).
```

Reference at the end of the paper
```
      Hughes, N. F. Palaeobiology of angiosperm
         origins: problems of Mesozoic seed-plant
         evolution. Cambridge Earth Science Series.
         London: Cambridge University Press, 1976b.
```

OVERVIEW OF
DOCUMENTATION STYLES:
ARTICLES

MLA Format (pp. 42–59)

LeGuin, Ursula K. "American Science Fiction and the Other." Science Fiction Studies 2 (1975):208-10.

Chicago Format (pp. 59–64)

Notes:

1. John Huntington, "Science Fiction and the Future," College English 37 (Fall 1975): 340-58.

Bibliography:

Huntington, John. "Science Fiction and the Future." College English 37 (Fall 1975): 340-58.

APA Format (pp. 114–122)

Miller, W. (1969). Violent crimes in city gangs. Journal of Social Issues, 27, 581-593.

CBE Number-Reference Format (See sample paper, p. 175–188)

1. Cotton, F. A. Photooxidation and photo-synthetic pigments. J. Cell. Biol. 87:32-43; 1987.

Author-Date Format (See sample paper, p. 191–204)

Dilcher, D. L.; Crepet, W. L.; Beeker, C. D.; Reynolds, H. C. Reproductive and vegetative morphology of a Cretaceous angiosperm. Science 191:854-856; 1976.

INDEX